Spiritual Dynamo

Spiritual Dynamo

Michael Faraday

Derick Bingham

CF4·K

**To Jonathan and Kimberly who always
listen so well to my stories.**

© Copyright 2006 Derick Bingham
ISBN: 978-1-84550-156-3
Reprinted 2010

Published by Christian Focus Publications,
Geanies House, Fearn, Tain, Ross-shire, IV20 1TW,
Scotland, Great Britain.
www.christianfocus.com
email: info@christianfocus.com

Cover Illustration by Fred Apps
Cover design by Andrea Raschemann

Printed and bound by Norhaven, Denmark

The facts in this book are accurate, but where necessary,
conversations have been imagined to aid the
telling of the story.

Contents

Switch on the Light

Every time you switch on a light, put in a plug, start up a computer or switch on a television, you do it because of discoveries related to the work of Michael Faraday.

If you fly in an aircraft through a lightning storm you will not be harmed because of something Michael Faraday understood. Even if you are in a huge modern ship you will be guided away from rocks by lighthouses whose powerful, penetrating light has been established because of help from Michael Faraday.

If you go for a swim in a swimming pool you will be guarded from disease because of liquid chlorine in the water: this is because Professor Faraday first liquefied chlorine.

Are you wearing a shirt or a dress that is coloured? It is because of discoveries about dye made by our hero. If you wear spectacles with lenses, eat your food with electroplated spoons, yes, Faraday has been involved. Once he discovered that electricity could be made by moving a magnet inside a coil of wire he was able to build the very first electric motor and later the first generator and transformer of electricity. This was in turn to light up cities like London, New York, Paris, Peking, and Moscow every night. Faraday's discovery was even to change long distance communication across the earth leading to the ability to talk to astronauts far out in space. When the British Prime Minister asked him of one of his discoveries, 'What good is it?' he replied. 'What good is a new-born baby?' By March 1860 reports of all Michael's investigations were numbered up to 16,041. Eventually through his investigations Michael influenced Albert Einstein and quantum physics. Einstein thought so much of Michael he kept a photograph of him on his study wall when working at Princeton University in the United States.

Professor Faraday was a genius who loved children. In 1826 he founded the soon-to-become-famous children's Christmas Lectures at the Royal Institution. His goal was to communicate to children the excitement of scientific discovery. Children just loved to hear him speak and packed out the lecture hall. A series of six of his children's lectures was published in 1860 as *The Natural History of a Candle* and it has become a classic of science literature. It has served as the basis for lessons in taking observations in science ever since.

Faraday discovered that an intense magnetic field could rotate the plain of polarised light. This is known today as the Faraday Effect and has guided the information about the magnetic fields of the galaxies. Put simply, this helps us understand what controls the alignment of interstellar dust particles!

Michael suffered from a disorder known as dyslexia. This meant that he had difficulty in learning to read or interpret words, letters, and other symbols. So it was that he spoke and wrote with difficulty. However, he overcame the problem to become one of the greatest public lecturers in history. He also had difficulty with mathematics but had a wonderful imagination. Many of his discoveries came through using his eyes in observing the world around him.

Apart from his life-long interest in science Michael was deeply interested in drawing and painting and in the methods of making prints and the development of photography. In his experiments he used instruments he had invented himself. Sometimes when he made a discovery he would write to an academic friend of his in Oxford and ask him to invent a name for the discovery he had made. This was because Michael had had only a very basic education and was raised on the edge of poverty.

At the age of fourteen he was apprenticed to a bookbinder and bookseller and began reading the books he was binding. The bookseller allowed him to use one of his rooms to carry out his own experiments.

When we think about it, because of what he discovered, much of what we experience in our modern world has been deeply influenced by Faraday. In his work *Twelve Books That Changed The World*, Melvyn Bragg chose Michael's book *Experimental Researches In Electricity* as one of those twelve books. He emphasises that Michael's work in his laboratory at the Royal Institute has changed the way we all live. He comments that from countless patient experiments Michael 'uncovered sources of energy from which we benefit every hour of the day; and in the three volumes he published are the proofs, written plainly for all.' He goes on to show that from Michael's discovery of benzene, for example, an understanding of all aromatics developed. So today we now have in a car 'the body, bumpers, lighting, dashboard, seats, upholstery, fuel systems and under-bonnet components' all derived from aromatics. He adds, 'Cumene and phenol - both derived from benzene - are key ingredients of aspirin and penicillin. CD's and DVD's are reliant on aromatics, as are plastic, acrylic and nylon for clothes.'

Michael Faraday was one of the greatest experimental scientists of all time and had one great and overwhelming characteristic above everything else in his life: he deeply loved and followed the Lord Jesus. He was totally unashamed of his devotion. On one occasion after a brilliant public lecture he had given at the Royal Institution on magnetism, the house 'rocked' with enthusiastic applause. The Prince of Wales who was present rose to propose public congratulations to the great Professor. The thunders of applause however, were followed by a strange silence. Everybody waited for Michael Faraday's reply, but the lecturer had vanished! Where was he? The truth was that the Professor was not just a great scientist, he was a great Christian and he had slipped away from the Royal Institution to be at his church's weeknight prayer meeting. He never missed the opportunity if it were possible to be there. His church never had more than twenty members but that didn't worry him. Having fellowship with God was as important to him as appearing before the most influential earthly audience. He also regularly visited the sick and the poor.

Michael Faraday believed that his great purpose in life was to read, as he put it, 'the book of nature … written by the finger of God'. Few people in history have read that book more accurately and applied it more helpfully. He is actually the only scientist to ever appear on the British £20 pound note. This is his incredible story.

Derick Bingham

Mike

'Mother! Mother!' shouted Robert Faraday as he burst through the front door of his home just north of Oxford Street in London.

'Calm down, son! Calm down!' said Margaret Faraday. 'Just tell me, slowly.'

'But Mother, you just won't believe what the teacher wanted me to do today. It was just awful!'

'What did she want you to do, son?' asked his mother now suddenly growing anxious as she saw the pained look on Robert's face.

'She offered me a half penny to buy a cane to thrash Mike!'

'Why, what has he done?' asked Margaret in surprise.

'He keeps calling me Wobert!'

'But that's because he has a speech defect,' said Mrs. Faraday. 'He can't help it if he is unable to pronounce words with a sounding 'r' in them.'

'I know, I know,' said Robert. 'But the horrible thing is that she wanted me to thrash it out of him.'

'What did you do?' asked Margaret Faraday in despair.

'I refused to do what she asked,' answered Robert. 'I threw the half penny over the wall and came home to tell you.'

'Well, you and Mike won't be going back to that school again,' said Mrs. Faraday. And they didn't.

The Faradays lived on the edge of poverty above a blacksmith's shop in the back premises of 16, Jacob's Mews. It was a bright and broad alley just north of Oxford Street in London that ran behind the Spanish Chapel of the Spanish Embassy. Mr. James Faraday, Michael and Robert's father was a blacksmith and he worked in the smithy below his rented rooms. He'd been a sick man for years and sometimes he was unable to complete a day's work. This meant that his family was not financially secure. At one stage in 1801 when England was at war with France and the price of corn was very high the young ten-year-old Michael was given a single loaf of bread that had to last him for a week.

James Faraday came from Clapham in North Yorkshire. He had married Margaret Hastwell, the sixth child of Michael and Betty Hastwell of Black Scar Farm at Kaber in Westmoreland at Kirby Stephen Parish Church in 1786. James took over a smithy opposite the King's Head Inn at Outhgill, five miles south of Kirby Stephen. Soon huge problems arose for James, Margaret and their two children Elisabeth and Robert. There was a drought in 1788 in the Mallerstang Valley of the River Eden where they lived.

'Let's pray for rain, Margaret,' James said to his wife one day as the drought increased. They both believed that God was interested in all the details and problems of their lives. They were convinced that he heard and answered prayer.

'We desperately need rain, James,' answered Margaret. 'The sheep and cattle are dying.'

'There isn't enough hay for the horses either,' said James. 'That means fewer coaches are coming up the valley and I am getting less work to do in shoeing horses.'

Soon the autumn with its frosts gave way to a very severe winter. For a period in December no coaches came up the valley at all and James had no work at the smithy. With summer came dramatic news from France.

'I hear a mob has stormed the Bastille prison in Paris, Margaret,' said James one summer day in 1789.

'What happened?' asked Margaret.

'The Bastille fortress surrendered,' answered James. 'And the mob freed the prisoners. The people danced and sang in the streets.'

'Will there by a wide-spread revolution in France?' asked Margaret anxiously.

'Looks like it' answered James. 'Poverty has driven the people to it. France hasn't got a proper Parliament like ours you know, and King Louis XVI is out-of-touch with the true conditions of his people.'

'Poverty drives a lot of people to do a lot of things, James,' said Margaret who was now experiencing what poverty meant for her little family. 'Do you think that England will go to war with France?'

'There is talk of it, Margaret, and I've seen soldiers on the move up and down the valley going to Carlisle, Leeds and London.'

'Maybe it's time for us to move, Margaret,' said James, after a period of thoughtful silence. 'We need to go to a city if I am to get work. I know you work hard as a maidservant at Deep Gill Farm but we need more money to care for Elisabeth and Robert. What do you think?'

'Let's go and talk to the elders of our Chapel and pray with them,' said Margaret.

God guides people through all kinds of circumstances. He over-rules even in the most difficult times. Just as the Bible shows that poverty drove Jacob to Egypt and drove the poverty-stricken Ruth to Israel, so God still over-rules events in peoples lives. James and Margaret decided to move as a family to the great metropolis of London. By the time they were ready to leave Outhgill, Margaret was heavily pregnant with a little baby. It was not an easy day for the Faradays when they left their home and all their friends in Westmoreland for an uncertain future in one of the largest cities on earth.

On September 22nd 1791 Margaret and James Faraday's little baby was born in rented rooms near the Elephant and Castle a short distance off the Old Kent Road in London. They called him Michael. He was to become a great, if not the greatest experimental scientist in history. If anyone was to prove the truth of the Bible verse that 'God has chosen the weak things of the world to put to shame the things which are mighty,' Michael Faraday was to be that person.

Not a lot is known of Michael's childhood but he did say later, 'My education was of the most ordinary description, consisting of little more than the rudiments of reading, writing and arithmetic at a common day-school.'

Times were very difficult and even the most basic education cost money. Michael's father would not have earned more than 20 shillings a week even at the best of times. Michael was actually very fortunate to even have received the education he did. When not at school Michael spent his time at home or playing in the streets. He was fond of playing marbles in nearby Spanish Place. He often looked after his little sister playing in Manchester Square.

'There's something about that boy,' his mother would say of him, 'he understands things immediately without having to reason it out.' She was right, for he had rare intelligence. 'My Michael!' she would say with deep affection when talking to others about him.

'I think it is time Michael went to work,' his father suggested to his wife when Michael was thirteen years of age. In the early 19th century family members were expected to contribute to family finances as soon as they were able.

'Well, he'll certainly make a good worker, James, for anyone fortunate enough to hire him,' said Margaret Faraday. She could not have been more right.

George Riebau ran a bookbinding and bookseller's shop just around the corner from Jabob's Mews at No 2. Blandford Street. He decided to hire Michael as an errand boy. It was busy work. His first task, early every morning, was to take newspapers round to all of Mr. Riebau's clients and then to visit them later in the day, collect the newspapers again and take them on to other clients. All the newspapers had to be returned after being read for which each client paid a small sum. These were days long before modern printing presses, telephones, television and satellites which, of course, Michael the errand boy was going to influence. Errand boys carrying newspapers around London were the main source of circulating news in the city.

News in 1801 was exciting. Lord Nelson with all his brilliance as a navy Commander led the British fleet to force the French fleet to surrender at the Battle of the Nile. He also led the action against the Danish fleet in the Battle of Copenhagen. Michael Faraday carried news of such battles as he rushed around London throughout the day.

'Faraday?' said Mr. Riebau one morning after Michael had worked for him for a year. 'I think you're going to be too bored running my errands for the rest of your youth. I think you would make an excellent bookbinder.'

'Really, sir?' answered a surprised Michael.

'Of course you would! I would like to offer you an apprenticeship to learn the trade of a bookbinder and stationer. It will be seven years of hard work and training but I am sure you would enjoy it and I would just love to have you here.'

'Can I talk to my parents about it,' said the excited fourteen-year-old boy.

'Of course,' answered Riebau.

On October 7th, 1805 Michael Faraday enthusiastically signed up as an apprentice bookbinder and stationer. On October 21st the most decisive sea battle of the Napoleonic wars was fought off Cape Trafalgar on the Spanish Coast between the combined fleets of Spain and France and the Royal Navy. Before the sun had set on that famous day Lord Nelson had been killed but his decisive command had brought victory and not one of the twenty-seven ships of the British Fleet had been sunk or captured. Napoleon's master plan to control the world through the command of the seas was shattered forever. It was not until several days after the battle that newspapers in England were able to inform their readers of its outcome. Michael Faraday, though, no longer carried the news. He was on his way to making it.

Little Things Lead to Big Things

'A thousand times without stopping, Faraday?' said George Riebau with amazement.

'Yes, that's true sir, I can strike one thousand blows with a hammer without resting,' answered Michael.

'Can't keep up with him, sir, he's like lightning,' said a fellow bookbinder raising his eyes to the ceiling in despair. 'He could hammer his way through a glacier, that one!'

Bookbinding was a skilful work and Michael Faraday responded with enthusiasm to all that George Riebau taught him. He learnt to trim pages sent in by the printer and he then mastered the skill of folding them. He also mastered the art of sewing pages. He cut hides and chose the right piece of leather for covering the book boards or book covers. He learned how to make glue from boiling wheat flower. Then he stuck the leather he had chosen to the book boards. He mastered the art of glazing a book cover with the beaten white of an egg, polishing it with a hot polishing iron. He enjoyed stamping the letters of the title of the book in gold leaf on the book spine. Bookbinding involved a lot of very detailed work.

'Faraday, you are different to other bookbinders,' George Riebau commented one day.

'How, sir?'

'You have a fascination for reading the books you are binding! Not everybody who handles books feels they have to read every word!'

'I love reading them, sir,' answered Michael. 'And what's more I love this book by Jane Marcet called *Conversations in Chemistry*.'

Michael Faraday was only fifteen when he first read Jane Marcet's book that had come in for binding. He later claimed that it gave him his first foundation in the science of chemistry. He said it was as 'the full light' in his mind.

Jane Marcet was a remarkable woman. She was born into a family of Swiss bankers. After an outstanding education she married a Swiss doctor and began to edit and proof read her husband's research. She became particularly interested in chemistry. She decided to write a book on the subject and wrote it in the form of questions between a teacher, Mrs. Brown and her two pupils, the impetuous Caroline and the more serious Emily. Her husband chose the themes and they repeated the main experiments together. Jane then wrote up each experiment in a series of conversations between the teacher and her pupils. She was able to teach the grand sweep of the science of chemistry without mathematics and it was just the very thing Michael Faraday needed.

Not only did Michael bind Jane's book and read it but also with the aid of jars and cooking pots he followed the experiments described in the book. Mr. Riebau generously gave him a room to carry out his experiments.

Jane Marcet's book *Conversations in Chemistry* became the most popular book on chemistry in the first half of the 19th century. It went into sixteen British and French editions during her lifetime. At least sixteen American editions were published. Jane also wrote books on philosophy and economics and wrote a book about Africa. Following the death of her husband she wrote a book called *Evidences of Christianity*. This book looked at the internal and external evidence that supports the fact that the writings of the New Testament are true. She would never have dreamt that she was to so deeply influence a fifteen-year-old teenager who was binding her book. She could not have imagined that he would become one of the greatest scientists in history. Jane and Michael were both firm believers in the stories and teachings of the Bible and God brought Jane's book and Michael's mind together for a great purpose.

Anyone passing No. 2 Blandford Street in London at night would have been amazed if they could have seen what the teenage Michael Faraday was up to. While his fellow workers were off enjoying themselves, Michael, with Mr. Riebau's encouragement, was copying the text and illustrations from the books in which he had been interested. This was his idea of pure pleasure. Hundreds upon hundreds of books were passing through the premises and the bookworm Michael was burrowing away gathering information to feed his hungry mind. While pursuing his ever-growing interest in science he was fascinated by an article in the Encyclopaedia Britannica on electricity. He even constructed an electrical machine, first with a glass phial and afterwards with a real cylinder.

During the day Riebau's bookshop was much more than a place where people went to buy books. London's bookshops were meeting places for the network of people in London who were radically opposed to the British king and the system of British government. Few monarchs in history have received more abuse than George III. Under his reign Britain lost her American colonies and eventually the unfortunate king descended into insanity. The fact is that he did attempt to rule fairly and it is unfair to just remember him only for his illness and for the loss of the colonies. He survived two assassination attempts. He and the Prime ministers who served under him had a whole movement opposed to them with publishers like George Riebau who published political pamphlets and literature.

Others who gathered at Blandford Street were people who strongly disagreed with the Church of England and not only political but also religious pamphlets were printed there. Mr. Riebau himself was a member of the Huguenot community that had fled France because of religious persecution. Mr. Riebau was sympathetic to a man called Emanuel

Swedenborg a scientist who had turned to writing deeply religious books. Mr. Riebau also wrote a book about a controversial character called Richard Brothers. Every day Michael was exposed to the discussions, debates and gossip of people who were out to change British society and some of whom were down right dangerous to know.

'I can see, Faraday, that you are interested in more than science,' said George Riebau on looking at Michael's copied illustrations. 'I think you should go and see the works of art which are exhibited at the Royal Academy.'

'Where is the Academy, sir?' asked Michael.

'It is round at Somerset House,' Mr. Riebau replied. 'You would truly enjoy the beautiful paintings there. They would inspire your own interest in art.'

Michael eventually went round to The Strand in London and passed through the magnificent entrance to Somerset House. The Royal Academy occupied apartments in Somerset House and had been founded by a group of artists headed by the portrait painter Joshua Reynolds. Here great artists like William Blake and J.M.W. Turner trained and here the leading artists of Britain exhibited their work at the famous Summer Academy. Michael also viewed the art at the British Institution in Pall Mall and George Riebau kindly went as far as asking his customers to let Michael see their private collections of art. Michael was to be deeply interested in art for the rest of his life.

While Michael was succeeding in his work, illness still continued to restrict and disturb the working life of his father. The work at the smithy was heavy and long and by 1807 James Faraday was off work for part of almost every day through the pain that he suffered. With his family's continued poverty, life for James was full of hardship.

There was one incident from his childhood that Michael always remembered, even as an adult. It highlighted the fact that his father had probably saved him from certain death.

'I was playing in an upstairs room above the smithy,' Michael would recall, 'when I stepped back from my game and fell through a hole in the rafters into the room below where my father was working at an anvil. My father's back just saved mine. If he'd not been working at the anvil I would have fallen upon it with serious if not fatal results.'

Sadly, in 1810, James Faraday died. He did not live to see Michael rise to worldwide fame. James Faraday once wrote to his brother in Yorkshire about his Christian faith that had stood firm in the midst of all the pain he suffered. He wrote about the overruling hand of the Sovereign God in human lives. His faith in Christ for salvation was a faith that was well placed.

The Faraday family had moved to Weymouth Street in London the year before James Faraday's death. These premises were much closer to George Riebau's shop and Mr. Riebau now took an even deeper interest in Michael's welfare seeking to be like a father to the fatherless teenager. He encouraged him to attend lectures given by a famous scientific lecturer and silversmith called John Tatum on Monday evenings.

'I'd like to go to Mr. Tatum's lectures, Robert,' said Michael to his brother one day.

'What are they about ?' asked Robert.

'Lots of interesting things,' answered Michael. 'Electricity, for example and geology, astronomy, chemistry, mechanics and optics. He covers most of science.'

'How much will it cost, Michael?' asked Robert.

'One shilling,' he answered.

'I'll find it for you,' answered Robert who was by now a working blacksmith.

It could not have been an easy task to find the money but Robert got it. How? We don't know but every Monday night Michael Faraday headed down to No. 53 Dorset Street just off Fleet Street in London able to pay his one shilling entrance fee. No blacksmith ever paid his precious money into a better investment for the good of all human kind. Michael would pay Robert back in terms far greater than the weekly shilling he found for him.

'My name is Benjamin Abbott,' said a fellow teenager one evening at the Tatum Lecture.

'Nice to meet you, Benjamin,' said Michael. 'My name is Michael Faraday. Do you enjoy it here?'

'I certainly do, Michael. I think it is just fantastic that Mr. Tatum can get through twenty to thirty experiments every Monday evening.'

'Last week's was a riot,' said Michael, laughing. 'That poor frog which had an electrical current pass through him and who hopped out of his jar into the audience certainly had a foot or two added to his usual leaps!'

'I loved the glass transparencies of landscape Mr. Tatum showed with the "magic lantern",' said Benjamin.

'Then there's how he shows water being decomposed by electricity,' said Michael.

John Tatum actually headed up an organisation called the City Philosophical Society of which the Monday evening lectures were a part. Michael became a member of the Society and slowly his confidence began to grow. Back at Blandford Street he made meticulous notes of Tatum's lectures including illustrated drawings. He even drew the lecture room in detail.

'A present for you, Mr. Riebau,' said Michael one day at work.

'Well, thank you,' said Mr. Riebau pulling back the paper wrapping from the gift. Inside he found four volumes of Michael's notes of Tatum's lectures, beautifully bound with a touching dedication thanking Mr. Riebau for permitting him to 'examine those books in your possession that were in any way related to the subjects then occupying my attention.' He signed it 'F. Maraday' by which he disguised his name. He did this for the rest of his life. There have been few scientists in history who have turned out to be as humble as Michael Faraday.

It is always fascinating to see the way God guides us. Sometimes He uses what might appear to be small incidents in our lives that can have incredible results. One of these was about to cross Michael's life. Michael continued to work hard in the Blandford Street bookshop, attended Tatum's lectures, and studied many books. When he was eighteen he began a collection of what he called 'Notices, Occurrences, Events etc. relating to the Arts and Science.' These he picked up from newspapers and magazines and other sources. While he did all of this work he became very aware of huge gaps in his education.

'Edward?' Michael asked another new friend he had made at the City Philosophical Society. 'Would you help me?' Edward Magrath was the Secretary of the Society.

'What can I do for you?' enquired his new friend eagerly.

'I desperately need to improve my grammar, punctuation and spelling,' said Michael.

'I'll give you tuition every week, if you like,' said Edward, generously.

'Thank you so much,' said Michael. 'It will really improve my writing. I make all these notes but my grammar is very weak.'

As it turned out, Edward Magrath gave Michael Faraday two hours tuition every week for seven years. His kind action shows that we all need each other. The great Apostle Paul's letters weren't much good without the help of his friend Tychicus to deliver them across many miles. The great surgeon needs the nurse to daily care for his patient. The world famous pianist is not much good without a piano tuner. A nail factory needs a hammer factory. The cracker maker will do better if there is a cheese maker. So Michael Faraday needed an Edward Magrath. He would not have become what he became without him.

All of this time Michael attended the church of his father and mother that met in a chapel in Paul's Alley, under the shadow of St. Paul's Cathedral in an area where very poor people lived. It was called a Sandemanian Chapel. The Scottish linen maker and Christian leader Robert Sandeman had founded this very tiny Christian denomination. At the services each member gave each other the kiss of peace and washed one another's feet as a sign of humility. They all ate together at the Chapel's spotless dining room between the morning and afternoon services on a Sunday. It was called a Love Feast. Otherwise they ate in each other's homes on Sundays. After communion was taken the members contributed money to the poor. All Sunday services began with a roll call and if members did not turn up they had to give a very good reason for it.

As Michael continued in his daily work he still found that faithfulness in little things led to much bigger things. When Mr. Riebau had lodgers in his house Michael had to blacken their boots and dust their rooms. However nothing seemed to have been wasted in his young life. One of Riebau's lodgers was a Frenchman called Jean-Jaques Masquerier who had fled to England from the French Revolution in 1798. Masquerier really liked Michael.

'Here, Michael,' he said. 'Have a look at these books on perspective.' Perspective is the art of conveying the height, width, depth, and relative distance of an object.

'I'd love to be able to draw perspective,' answered Michael.

'I'll teach you to draw,' said Masquerier. So it was that Michael's notebooks on Tatum's Lectures contained detailed perspective drawings of all kinds of apparatus used by the lecturer.

When George Riebau showed Michael's notebooks to one of his customers, a man called George Dance, it resulted in one of the major turning points of his life.

As we have already noted, God constantly uses small incidents to bring about incredible ends. George Dance was so impressed with the standard of Michael's work that he asked if he could borrow the books to show to his father William. George Dance was a brilliant architect and his father was a musician.

All the members of the Dance family were members of the Royal Institution that met in a very fashionable mansion on Albemarle Street in London. The Institute had been established in 1799 'for teaching, by means of philosophical lectures and experiments, the application of science to the common purposes of life.'

'I've been sent a ticket, Mr. Riebau,' said Michael with great excitement one morning at his work.

'What for, Faraday?' asked his interested employer.

'It came from Mr. Dance and it is a pass to attend the remaining lectures of Sir Humphry Davy,' said Michael, 'at the Royal Institution.'

'What a wonderful opportunity, Michael!' said Mr. Riebau. 'You must go. There are a thousand people who cram in there to listen to every lecture. You must, you simply must go.'

Michael headed for Albemarle Street and the world has never been quite the same since.

Fire-lighter, Sweeper and Washer

There were hundreds of people heading down Albemarle Street under the stars. It was Leap Year night 29th February 1812 and the crowds of people were in a hurry and full of excited conversation. Michael Faraday listened carefully as he walked along with them.

'Did you see Professor Davy demonstrate that Laughing Gas,' said one lady wearing ostrich feathers in her fashionable hat. 'I was present on that night.'

'I did, I did,' said her acquaintance. 'As soon as the man from the audience breathed that nitrous oxide coming from that silk bag and down that tube he was intoxicated. He jumped about all over the lecture theatre platform and fell about laughing. They say the gas gives a tingling in your toes and fingers.'

'I've heard it said that one day dentists will use it as an anaesthetic for pulling teeth,' said the first lady as she jostled in the crowd.

'Wish they'd hurry and use it,' retorted her acquaintance. 'I hate the dentist's chair.'

'I hear Napoleon Bonaparte has awarded Professor Davy a medal for his work on electromagnetism,' said another man as Michael neared the Royal Institution Headquarters.

'Our war with France must mean that the Professor can't collect it,' said his companion.

As Michael heard the people talk around him he began to wonder what the coming lecture would be like. The man he was about to listen to came from Penzance in Cornwall. He had risen from being an apprentice to a surgeon and apothecary to becoming Professor of chemistry at the Royal Institution. Affectionate, cheerful, quick-witted Professor Davy had a very lively imagination. He loved to write poetry, sketch, shoot, make fireworks and collect minerals. He loved to go for long walks particularly where there were mountains and water. Probably his greatest passion was for fishing. He made his own fishing tackle and sets of hooks. He created his own flies for trout fishing with thread and bits of brightly coloured feather. He even designed a green cloth fisherman's suit for himself with many pockets. He owned a pair of rubber boots that came up to his knees and when he went shooting he covered his hat with scarlet cloth so that nobody would shoot at him!

When Michael Faraday heard Humphry Davy speak in February 1812, Davy was three months away from marriage and from being Knighted by the Prince Regent. He was giving his last series of ten public lectures (Michael attended four) at the Royal Institution and was at the very height of his fame as a public lecturer. People hung on his every word and his carefully prepared and rehearsed lectures had become very important social functions in London. He had lifted the study of science to new heights.

'I like to sit in the balcony, as you know Michael,' said George Dance as he accompanied the eager young nineteen-year-old bookbinder into the Royal Institution. 'Right above the clock.'

'And I like to make notes!' said Michael.

'That tall hat of yours is a most useful desk,' said George, smiling.

Michael put his tall black hat on his knees and placed the folds of paper he had brought with him on top of the hat. He held his pencil at the ready. He eagerly waited for the great chemist to appear. He was not disappointed. With a bright smile, the curly-headed, good-looking Professor strolled onto the platform of the lecture hall. Michael watched, mesmerised as Professor Davy shone a white light out of a lamp onto a prism where the light split in the colours of the rainbow and then passed through other prisms and lenses to come back again as a white light to illuminate a sheet of card. Professor Davy then sprinkled black powder onto a pan of red-hot charcoal. There was an explosion, a flash and a very violent hiss, and bits of charcoal scattered across the bench.

'Goodness!' shrieked a woman near the front.

'Thought my time had come just then!' laughed a man near Michael.

The Professor then explained what had been happening.

'What did you think of him tonight, Michael?' asked George Dance when the lecture was over and they jostled with the crowd down Albemarle Street.

'Superb!' answered Michael, 'I think this is a great series. He makes science fascinating. I also love the Cornish burr in his accent, too!'

It is worth noting that Michael was truly blessed with good friends at this time in his life. George Dance for example, was a thoughtful and helpful friend to him. George was to become Architect and Surveyor to the Corporation of London and his most important works would include the rebuilding of Newgate Prison, the designs of St. Luke's Hospital and the front of London's Guildhall. He became Professor of Architecture at the Royal Academy. He is also famous for 200 drawings of his friends and contemporaries that he sketched from life including Lord Castlereagh and James Boswell.

Within the next few months Michael was to need his friends. 'The most important of my discoveries have been suggested by my failures,' Professor Davy once said. Michael now faced a failure. Knowing that within six months his apprenticeship as a bookbinder to George Riebau would end, he was absolutely determined to follow a life of science. Humphry Davy had particularly inspired him and one summer day in 1812 he walked back up The Strand and through the fine entrance to Somerset House. This time he headed for the rooms of the Royal Society and approached the porter.

'Could you possibly give this letter to Sir Joseph Banks?' said Michael rather gingerly.

'Certainly, Sir,' replied the porter.

'I'll call for an answer in two to three days,' said Michael, as he departed.

Within two to three days Michael returned and asked 'Please could you tell me if there is any reply to the letter I gave you recently?'

'Sorry, Sir,' said the porter looking through the papers at his desk. 'There is nothing here for you.'

'Are you sure?' asked a disappointed Michael.

'I'm sure,' he replied.

Sir Joseph Banks was the President of the Royal Society of London, probably the most prestigious scientific organisation of the time. Sir Joseph had been a very famous explorer having sailed with Captain James Cook around the world on his ship *The Endeavour* to discover uncharted lands in the South Pacific. He had a passion for botany and collected thousands of plant specimens and brought them back to Europe. He was with Captain Cook when he made landfall at Botany Bay in Australia. He became an Honorary Director of the Royal Botanic Gardens at Kew. Sir Joseph also made the arrangements for sending Captain William Bligh to collect breadfruit plants for the West Indies. It was hoped that breadfruit would be grown in the West Indies to feed the slaves. Captain Bligh's voyage is now best known for the mutiny under Fletcher Christian on H.M.S. Bounty in April 1789. Captain Bligh and seventeen of his loyal crew members were set adrift in an open boat. By skilful seamanship Bligh navigated three thousand six hundred and sixty eight miles back to civilisation.

Michael had asked Sir Joseph in his letter for work at the Royal Society, any kind of work, even bottle washing, if possible. He kept calling back again, day after day for about ten days hoping that Sir Joseph would respond.

'A message for you, sir,' said the porter when on yet another occasion the young bookbinder arrived at his desk.

'Sir Joseph Banks has asked me to tell you that your letter requires no answer.'

Michael was so disappointed it did not seem that any of his friends could comfort him.

'Michael, there will be other opportunities for you,' said George Riebau. 'You must not give up.'

'Life does not stop for you just because the big-headed Sir Joseph Banks says "no",' Edward Magrath sympathised. 'He has been so carried away by his position and fame he has missed an opportunity to have a worker at the Royal Society who would be one of his best. But remember Michael, in the middle of difficulty lies opportunity.'

'Ah, come on Michael,' said George Dance. 'Come on. Those wonderful drawings and notes of yours show that you have real talent. When God shuts a door, he opens a window. Fly out that window, Michael, fly.'

'Fly where? Mr. Dance, fly where?' said Michael. 'Sir Joseph Banks wouldn't even have me as a bottle washer!'

'Well, then, send Sir Humphry Davy the notes and drawings of his last four lectures that you are currently working on.'

For Michael the summer of 1812 passed busily despite his discouragement. He continued to write up Sir Humphry Davy's lecture notes and he worked at home and at the back of Riebau's shop building a battery. He also carried on making experiments using his own apparatus. Michael has left on record that at this time he was deeply influenced by a book written by the great English hymn writer Dr. Isaac Watts called *The Improvement of the Mind*. The man who wrote the famous hymn *When I Survey the Wondrous Cross* and the lovely Christmas hymn *Joy to the World* had also written *The Improvement of the Mind*. It was on the subject, as he put it, of 'communication of useful knowledge in religion, in the sciences, and in common life.' The book had come in to Riebau's for binding and selling. In it Michael states that Dr. Watts had urged upon young people the usefulness of letter writing for improving the mind. Michael decided to put Dr. Watt's advice into practice.

'I think Dr. Watts is right,' he said to his friend Benjamin Abbott one evening when they met to discuss science at one of their weekly meetings. 'I think you and I should write each other letters exchanging our knowledge and the results of experiments we do. It will help improve our minds and make us express our ideas clearly and distinctly.'

'What a good idea, Michael,' replied Benjamin. 'I think it would be a pity not to write down what we have learned. When do you think we should start?'

'Right away,' replied Michael, enthusiastically. 'We'll keep the post busy between your house here in Bermondsey and my house in Weymouth Street.'

They did just that for the best part of ten years! Today Michael Faraday's letters are published by the Institution of Electrical Engineers in six volumes edited by Frank A.J.L. James. A flavour of what those letters contain can be gained from the following letter written by Michael to Benjamin Abbott on the 2nd and 3rd August 1912.

'What is the longest, and the shortest thing in the world: the swiftest and the most slow: the most divisible and the most extended: the least valued and the most regretted: without which nothing can be done: which devours all that is small: and gives life and spirits to everything that is great!

'It is that, Good Sir, the want of which has until now delayed my answer to your welcome letter. It is what the Creator has thought of such value as never to bestow on us mortals two of the minutest portions of it at once. It is that which with me is at the instant very pleasingly employed. It is Time.'

The summer of 1812 was a wet one. It found Michael, though, spending time gazing at the stars through an astronomical telescope. He even found time to go with Benjamin to the firework concerts at the new Ranelagh Gardens in Millbank. He also survived a serious incident when a boat he was in nearly sank after hitting Battersea Bridge. On September 22nd at twenty-one years of age Michael found himself out of work. His apprenticeship with George Riebau was over. In seeking employment he now took up a position as a bookbinder with Henry de la Roche of King Street, Portman Square in London. He was truly unhappy. His employer was a bad tempered individual and Michael found the world of bookbinding too restrictive. He was determined to follow science and at times he would call on George Riebau telling him how he wished he could be introduced to Sir Humphry Davy. Riebau gave him the same advice as George Dance:

'Send him the bound copies of your notes and drawings of his lectures, Michael, they are brilliant. Write a covering letter. Leave them with him for examination.'

'I'm nervous, Mr. Riebau,' answered Michael. 'Sir Joseph Banks wouldn't even have me as a bottle washer.'

'But how will Sir Humphry know about you if you don't tell him?' answered Riebau.

One day in late October Michael decided to act on his two friends' advice and send his manuscripts and drawings to Sir Humphry Davy. To his great joy the very next morning a footman from Sir Humphry arrived requesting that Michael come and see him.

'Mr. Faraday,' said Sir Humphry, on meeting the bookbinder for the first time. 'I advise you to stay with your book binding for the time being, but if any opportunity arises I will consider you for employment. Thank you for your notes and drawings. They are just excellent. It was good of you to send them to me.'

The opportunity arose sooner than Sir Humphry expected. In late October he was mixing ammonium nitrate and chlorine in an experiment in the laboratory of a fellow scientist called John Children at Tunbridge Wells in Kent when there was an explosion. The glass tube containing the chemicals shattered and a piece of glass went into Sir Humphry's eye damaging it badly. Sir Humphry sent for Michael and asked if he would do some work for him as his sight had been affected. On some days when he was not with Henry de la Roche, Michael helped Sir Humphry and as Christmas Eve 1812 settled across the great city of London, he wrote him a letter that Michael always treasured. He commended Michael for his zeal, power of memory, and attention. He also told him he would be pleased to be of service to him.

If an explosion had caused Sir Humphry to first turn to Michael for some help, a fight brought Michael even closer. The scene unfolded at the Royal Institution lecture theatre about six and a half weeks later.

A man called William Payne who was a laboratory assistant to the new Professor of chemistry at the Royal Institution who had succeed Sir Humphry, failed to do his job properly. The instrument maker at the Royal Institution, John Newman turned to William Payne in the lecture theatre on February 19th and said:

'William, I am sorry to have to tell you but your work has not been good recently. The new chemistry Professor, Professor Brande is a real stickler for detail and he expects all his instruments, chemicals and illustrations to be in place. You failed him this week and I really have to reprimand you.'

'And who do you think you are, Newman, talking to me like that?' said Payne. 'You make your instruments and I'll attend to my laboratory work as I see fit.'

'But I am only doing my duty pointing out to you that it is unfair to Professor Brande to be left in the lurch because of you.'

'Shut up, Newman,' cried Payne.

'I will not shut up. You must do better,' shouted Newman.

'I'll shut you up then,' said Payne and drew out and hit the instrument maker. There was a cry of pain as Newman reeled from the violent punch that had just injured him. The two men brawled so noisily the Superintendent of the Royal Institution rushed to investigate and in assessing the situation charged Payne with hitting Newman. Payne went away cursing the Superintendent and three days later, after ten years of service, William Payne was sacked.

Somebody was now needed to take William Payne's place. Poor Michael had been in a dark tunnel of frustration for some time. He bitterly disliked working for Henry de la Roche and even though his employer had offered to transfer his business to Michael, he had refused. Michael knew that the volatile nature of Henry de la Roche could cause him to lose his bookbinding job and he would be plunged into poverty. His mother Margaret depended on him to give her extra money to keep the family home together. Where was the light in this tunnel?

Late on the evening of February 22nd 1813 a shiny carriage wheeled into Weymouth Street, London. It stopped at No. 18 and a smartly dressed footman climbed down from the box by the driver and gave a firm rap on the door. Michael was upstairs at that moment getting ready for bed and he was suddenly aware of a conversation going on downstairs.

'Could you please give this letter to Mr. Michael Faraday,' said the footman.

'Is it urgent?' said the door opener.

'Yes. If you could give it to him right away I'd be much obliged. It is from Sir Humphry Davy, the Honorary Professor of chemistry at the Royal Institution.'

The shiny carriage moved out of Weymouth Street into the darkness but Michael Faraday was about to move on out of the tunnel he was in to a whole new bright horizon in his life. And all through a bit of glass and a fight! When Michael opened the letter he found a request from Sir Humphry Davy to call upon him at the Royal Institution the next morning.

Michael got up the next morning and excitedly headed out for the Royal Institution – now recognised as the oldest independent research body in the world. He walked up Albemarle Street and into the Royal Institution passing to the anti-room of the lecture theatre where he had first been enchanted by Professor Davy's lectures.

'Good morning Mr. Faraday. I trust I have not inconvenienced you by inviting you to come to see me so quickly,' said Sir Humphry.

'Not at all, Sir Humphry,' said Michael, who had not been able to get to Albemarle Street quickly enough!

'Tell me, do you still feel the same way about helping me here at the Royal Institution as you did last year?'

'I certainly do,' replied Michael.

'I'm delighted to hear it Mr. Faraday, because this morning I am in a position to offer you the situation of Assistant in the Laboratory of the Royal Institution in the place of Mr. William Payne who was lately employed here. Would you be in a position to accept the offer?'

Michael rose to shake Sir Humphry's hand with sheer delight.

'Of course, Sir Humphry, nothing would give me greater pleasure. Thank you so much for considering me.'

No happier man ever walked up Albemarle Street than Michael Faraday on September 23rd 1813. He was officially appointed as 'fire-lighter, sweeper, apparatus cleaner and washer' at the Royal Institution. He had, though, on negotiation, been provided with a regular supply of aprons, the use of laboratory apparatus for his own experiments, two attic rooms at 21 Albemarle Street, as much coal and candles for heat and light as he needed and a salary of one guinea per week. Within a week he was helping Sir Humphry with an experiment seeking to extract sugar from sugar beet.

'The reason for this experiment, Mr. Faraday is because of a danger that threatens this nation from France,' said Sir Humphry. 'If Napoleon's fleet blockades our ports we will not be able to import sugar from the West Indies.'

Michael had certainly moved on from bookbinding. He was deeply happy amongst glass tubes, acids, gases, troughs of water, acrid smoke, stinks, bottles, retorts, glass stoppers, and brass taps. He was working with one of the greatest teachers in his nation and even experienced many explosions from the chemicals they were mixing! Wearing glass masks and often ducking down behind the bench to try to escape from the unpredictable results of their experiments Michael did not in fact, entirely escape. On one occasion he nearly had his hand blown apart.

Michael even wrote to his friend Benjamin Abbott describing his work in helping to make a new explosive which would eventually be used by fighting armies called nitrogentrichloride.

***

'Michael, I have a proposal for you, and I'm afraid I haven't been able to give you much of a warning,' said Sir Humphry one morning.

'What do you have you in mind, Sir Humphry?' asked Michael curiously.

'The Emperor Napoleon and the Institut de France have given me a medal for my work on electrochemistry. I would like to go to France to collect it. I know that our nation is at war with France but we scientists are not at war and I have been given a special passport for me and my party to go. Lady Jane and I and our party hope to make a tour to France, Switzerland, Germany, Italy, Greece and Turkey lasting about two to three years. Would you be interested in joining us as my Assistant?

Drawing breath Michael looked into the eyes of the great scientist before him and gently said, 'It would be new territory for me, Sir Humphry. I have never travelled more than ten miles from the centre of London in my entire life. But I would love the opportunity of going with you. It would be quite a journey.'

He didn't realise just what an amazing journey it would turn out to be.

The Man who had Never Seen the Sea

Anyone walking down Grosvenor Street in London on the morning of October 13th 1813 would have seen a lot of activity outside Sir Humphry Davy's house. A shining black carriage stood by the pavement with restless horses in their traces, raring to be off. All kinds of shapes and sizes of travelling trunks were being loaded up.

'Mr. Faraday, you're to join me on the roof with the driver,' said Humphry Davy's footman. 'It may be cold up there but you'll have a first class view of the journey.'

'Suits me fine,' answered Michael. 'I've never been ten miles from the centre of London in my entire life.'

'Time you widened your horizons Mr. Faraday,' said the driver. 'We shall pass through some beautiful countryside.'

Michael was on his way to one of the greatest adventures of his life. He was to travel for the next eighteen months through France, over the Alps to Genoa, Turin, Florence, Siena, Rome, Naples, then into Switzerland and Germany and back to Italy again before returning to his home in London. He was to meet some of Europe's greatest scientists.

First, though, it was out of Grosvenor Street and a brisk trot down Park Lane and round Hyde Park corner into Kensington and out towards Kew. The carriage swayed with its heavy load of trunks and while Sir Humphry and Lady Davy viewed the passing scene from the comfort of the inside of their carriage, Michael surveyed the scene from the wind-swept roof. He was mesmerised as his eyes watched London recede and a whole new world opened to his ever-astute and discerning eyes.

Michael kept a journal of his journey and that is how we now know in detail what he saw, felt, and experienced. First they travelled to Amesbury just north of the city of Salisbury. The next day the carriage rolled along the edge of Salisbury Plain and Michael saw Stonehenge for the first time as they passed close by. The second day they got to Exeter and spent the night at an inn under the shadow of the Cathedral.

'Faraday,' snapped Lady Jane the next morning. 'Please attend to Sir Humphry's shaving immediately. And his clothes were not laid out as neatly as I would have expected this morning,' she added.

'Immediately, Lady Humphry,' answered Michael. 'And I'll make sure I lay Sir Humphry's clothes out in a more orderly fashion tomorrow morning.'

Lady Jane Humphry was a very irritable individual and treated servants in a very abrupt and off-hand manner. Michael Faraday got the worst of her treatment. He had agreed to be Sir Humphry's valet until a replacement could be found in Paris. A valet is a man's personal male attendant, responsible for his clothes and appearance. Michael, who did not find Lady Jane an easy person to deal with by any means, discovered that she also had a mind numbing habit: she virtually never stopped talking. This habit drove Michael to distraction.

The next day they journeyed round the southern edge of a very famous moorland called Dartmoor. Michael wrote that he had been more taken by its scenery than anything else he had ever seen. Here were wooded, sheltered valleys and great wind-swept granite tors or rocky peaks weathered into curious shapes over many thousands of years. Dartmoor is, in fact, the jewel of the famous West Country of England and Michael saw the beautiful moorland landscape sparkle. That evening Sir Humphry Davy's party arrived at the port of Plymouth where the River Tamar empties into Plymouth Sound and the English Channel.

The Port of Plymouth has seen some very famous voyagers set sail from her harbour. From here Sir Francis Drake had sailed in November 1577 in the Golden Hind to become the first Englishman to circumnavigate the globe. On July 20th 1588 the vast Spanish Armada had appeared off Plymouth. It consisted of 130 ships manned by about 8,000 sailors and more than 19,000 soldiers with mules and horses and enough wine and ships biscuits to last half a year. Sir Francis Drake and other famous seamen of the age sailed against the Spanish and the Spanish were soundly defeated. From this very port the Pilgrim Fathers sailed on *The Mayflower* for America. Sir Humphry Davy and his party had arrived at Plymouth in a time of war and they hoped to sail for France the next day on a cartel.

'What is a cartel?' Michael asked the coach driver as they entered Plymouth.

'It's a specially licensed ship in time of war, Mr. Faraday,' answered the coach driver. 'It is allowed to carry mail, messages and prisoners for exchange. It is allowed free passage by both warring sides. Let's hope we can sail in the morning, but I don't like the look of the weather, the wind is really getting up. What do you think of the sea, then, Mr. Faraday?'

'Wonderful. Just wonderful!' said Michael who had only lived in a great city for twenty-two years and had never seen the sea before. 'I just can't wait to sail.'

The coachman was right. The wind continued to howl across Plymouth Sound and they could not sail that day. The next day, Sunday October 17th, the Captain of the cartel decided all was in order, the carriage was now stowed in pieces on the ship and the entire luggage had been loaded. He hoped to sail with the tide.

'We need some English money changed into French francs, Captain,' insisted Sir Humphry Davy. He was told that there was a problem. The Jewish moneychangers of Plymouth refuse to do business until after sunset. It was the ninth day of the Jewish Feast of Tabernacles.

'Ah we'll get around that problem,' chuckled the Captain, who unfortunately was not averse to cheating. 'I'll put my watch forward. Here, let us close these shutters.' He then proceeded to light some candles. 'Go and bring those moneychangers in,' he requested.

When the moneychangers arrived with their bags of French francs the Captain warmly greeted them. 'Ah! Gentlemen, welcome,' he said. ' As you can see it is now past sunset. Can we get down to business?'

Just as one of the moneychangers reached for his money bag his wife walked in and warned him that the hour was too early. The sun had not set. The game was up!

So it was that Sir Humphry and his party had to kick their heels for a while longer waiting impatiently for the sun to set. The Captain, meanwhile, took his ship out of Plymouth Harbour on the evening tide and waited on Plymouth Sound. Eventually the money was changed and the Davys' and their party rushed down to the quayside, clambered into a little sailing boat and sailed out into the Sound and climbed on board the cartel ship.

Michael stayed on deck all night. He paced up and down the deck entranced by his first sea voyage. The seabird's call, the sea-salt spray, the stars high above him, the sound of the sea waves as the ship's bow cut into them giving off a phosphorescent luminous light, captured his imagination. He sat at times wrapped in a blanket watching it all. Then he would rise and lean on the ships rail gazing down into the water as the ship rose and fell on the sea waves, mountains and valleys of water all around him.

The cartel ship made landfall at Morlaix on the Brittany coast the next evening, but it was too late to disembark. The ship anchored for the night and Michael spent another night on deck. The next morning the ship lifted its anchor and sailed up the Dossem Channel, which forms the port of Morlaix. The town lies between four to five miles from the English Channel and the cartel, flying a flag of truce, sailed past the old fortress of the Chateaux de Taueau and the French ship guarding entry to the Dossem Channel. The cartel eventually weighed anchor in the harbour.

'Ah! Mr. Faraday, will you ever get to land?' bantered the cabin boy. 'These Frenchies are the dickens for being slow. I think you could have written quite a few letters by the time they get here.'

'You're a rascal,' answered Michael, laughing. He had in fact written a letter home and was feeling quite a tinge of homesickness. He was also hiding his fear of the enemy, France. Eventually a barge full of Frenchmen arrived at the side of the cartel and everyone on board was questioned and searched. Michael's pockets, clothes, and even his hat were thoroughly searched.

'Take your shoes off,' snapped the French Official to Michael. 'I need to be sure there are no secret messages hidden in them.'

'And could we have that letter you were writing,' he continued. 'You are not permitted to write home about your arrival and reception in France. If you do you risk being arrested as a spy.'

The luggage and the carriage pieces along with the passengers were now all loaded onto the barge and the cartel sailed away for England. Michael was sorry to see it go. The barge unfortunately stuck in the mud of the Dossem Channel as the tide flowed out. Would they ever get to land? They waited and waited. Slowly the moon rose and eventually the barge refloated with the incoming tide. They tied up at Morlaix Quay and walked on foot to the town's only hotel.

'It can't possibly be a hotel,' said Sir Humphry in disgust. 'I've just seen a horse go through the front door!'

'I'm afraid it is a hotel,' answered Michael. 'It must be like a pigsty inside.'

That is exactly what it was like, but tired out by their exhausting voyage they all found what comfort they could in sleep. The next day, though, was equally exhausting. Soldiers marched up and down the edge of the quay while several dozen locals clattered down the quay steps and started unloading the Davy party's luggage.

'Somebody is going to break their neck,' said Sir Humphry as the men started to lift the carriage pieces by hand.

'Disgusting fellows,' snapped Lady Jane, as she watched the proceedings. 'We'll be very fortunate to have a carriage at all at the end of all this.'

Eventually, all their possessions were taken to the Custom House and every single one was laid out on tables. The authorities even tried to confiscate a few dozen cotton stockings until Sir Humphry gave them some money as a bribe and they returned the stockings. Even when the carriage was assembled and their possessions returned there was a further delay. The authorities needed to check, they said, if the Government still allowed Sir Humphry his passport to visit France. If not, they would all be prisoners immediately! They waited one more day at the disgustingly foul hotel where not only horses entered but pigs and poultry passed by the gilded chairs and tables in the dining room.

At long last their carriage and horses were ready for travelling. The postillion, the person who rides the leading near side horse of a team of horses pulling a carriage, got onto his horse, the driver cracked his whip with its six foot thong above the heads of the horses and they were off to Paris.

Little seemed to escape the eye of the ever-watchful Michael. Outside the city of Rennes the gateway to the Breton Peninsula, a horse stumbled and broke away from its traces. As the postillion tried to calm the horses and get things back in order, Michael didn't waste a moment.

'Look at this,' he said to the footman. 'Look what I found. I found a worm that glows!' In fact the glow-worm is a beetle and only the wingless female glows strongly. She does this to attract male beetles and only has a glowing life of a few weeks until she mates. She dies soon after laying her eggs.

'Quite a phenomenon Mr. Faraday,' said the footman, intrigued by the young Faraday who found everything around him so interesting, including glow-worms!

The long journey to Paris improved as the roads improved. Napoleon was a ruthless dictator but he did try to set up improvements in the public work systems in France. There were less bumps and ruts on the now straighter roads into Paris and soon the carriage stopped in the Square outside the Palace of Versailles in order that the horses might be changed for the journey into Paris. As they waited Sir Humphry Davy explained the significance of the palace:

'This magnificent palace started out as a hunting lodge for Louis XIII,' he said, looking up. 'When his son Louis XIV, known as the Sun King lived here, it became the official residence of the Court and Government of France. Can you imagine, Faraday, what it was like here when a great mob of people from Paris marched to Versailles during the recent revolution and forced the late Louis XVI and his wife Marie Antionette to return the dozen and more miles to Paris with them. What a grizzly end they had by execution! Did you know Faraday, that while Marie Antionette lived here she had a miniature village built nearby, complete with mill and church, and she and her friends, tired of the stiff, formal and boring life of the French court – played at being ordinary country folk. No wonder there was a revolution!'

The further journey into Paris ended in the Rue de Richelieu in Paris. As the carriage pulled up at the Hotel des Princes, Michael, who went in first to check that everything was prepared for Sir Humphry and his party was staggered by its sumptuousness. He gazed on the marble-topped furniture, bright lights and panelled walls and thought that a greater contrast to the hotel in Morlaix simply could not have been found. The hotel, however, was to become a historic part of the discovery of an amazing substance over the following weeks.

Over the Hills and Far Away

'Get me to a window quickly, Monsieur, quickly!' cried Nicolas Clément the distinguished French scientist. 'My eyes are stinging!'

'I'm choking, Monsieur Davy, I'm choking!' cried a distressed André-Marie Ampère, another of France's leading scientists as he stumbled towards the window of the Hotel des Princes.

A poisonous, violet coloured smoke had filled the room after Sir Humphry had heated a few flakes of a strange black substance. It had been brought to him by the scientists for investigation. They did not know what it was. It had first been noticed in crystal form in France when a gun powder manufacturer had been producing potassium nitrate.

'Ah! Fresh air, Monsieur,' said a relieved Charles Desormes one of the three scientists who had brought Sir Humphry Davy the strange by-product of gunpowder.

'How did you get this substance?' asked Sir Humphry when the air had cleared.

'We're not allowed to tell you, Monsieur,' answered André-Marie Ampère. 'It is a secret because of national security in this time of war.'

Despite having just filled the room with thick violet coloured smoke, Sir Humphry now took a few more flakes of the strange substance and heated them in a sealed jar. The same smoke appeared but when the substance cooled it formed purple crystals around the neck of the jar.

'Let me rub the substance with zinc filings,' said Sir Humphry with authority as Michael stood behind him taking in all that was happening.

'Look,' said Charles Desormes. 'A liquid is forming.'

'Stand back,' warned Sir Humphry as he now put some of the substance into a tube and mixed it with potassium. The mixture immediately flared up.

'It's changing colour,' said Nicolas Clément in surprise. The substance had now been mixed with mercury and it changed from orange to black and then to red.

'Be careful, Monsieur Davy,' warned Charles Desormes. 'If the hotel authorities catch you doing these dangerous experiments they might put you out of the hotel.'

'It would be worth it if I could find out what this strange substance actually is,' answered Sir Humphry.

For most of the rest of his stay in Paris Sir Humphry Davy continued experimenting with what the French scientists had called 'Substance X.' All sorts of strange smells came wafting out of the door of his hotel room. Bangs and 'whooshing' noises could be heard daily. Over at the Jardin des Plantes in the laboratory of the French scientist Michel Chevreul, Sir Humphry and Chevreul worked on the substance together with Michael keeping meticulous notes of all that was going on. Eventually Sir Humphry came to the conclusion that the substance was not a mixture of chemical elements but was itself an individual chemical element closely related to chlorine, another chemical element Sir Humphry had been responsible for isolating. He called the mysterious substance 'Iodine' from the Greek word for 'violet-like.'

Iodine actually occurs in sea water and is taken in by sea weeds from which it may be recovered. It is found in many other sources including Chilean salt-petre which was actually the substance that the French gunpowder manufacturer had been working with. It is also found in salt wells. It is absolutely essential for our health. Too low or too high intake of iodine in human beings can cause forgetfulness, personality change, and depression as well as dry, scaly skin. Eating cabbage, brussel sprouts, broccoli, and cauliflower can aid our iodine intake.

On the days that Michael was not engaged in helping Sir Humphry with his scientific work he was free to explore Paris. He walked many miles often having to leap away from cabriolets, the light two-wheeled, hooded carriages pulled by single horses and driven furiously by Parisian men. There were no footpaths and his feet often became sore walking on the small sharp stones on the street surface.

One day he had to present himself at the Prefecture of Police opposite the great Notre Dame

Cathedral. He had to apply for a passport for internal travel in France. He knew practically no French and discovered he had to pay for information as to which office was the one he needed. When he found it the room was filled with twenty desks, each one with a clerk sitting behind it with an enormous ledger. There were twenty long queues of people waiting to be dealt with. Poor Michael couldn't make himself understood and hundreds of people started to stare at him. He was deeply embarrassed. What could he do?

'Hi buddy, can I be of any help?' said a cheerful American voice.

'I would be very grateful for some help sir,' said Michael. 'I am applying for a passport.'

'And you an enemy Englishman!' laughed the American. The French, of course, had fought with the Americans against Britain in the American War of Independence. Twenty years before on September 3rd 1783 the British had recognised American Independence by signing the Treaty of Paris.

'I'm actually here in France with Sir Humphry Davy the eminent scientist,' replied Michael. 'Napoleon has given us special treatment.'

The American explained Michael's story to the clerk behind the huge ledger at the top of Michael's queue.

'You and Sir Humphry Davy are the only two free Englishmen in the whole of Paris at the moment,' said the clerk.

'Wow, buddy, you are privileged!' said the American, slapping Michael on the back as he went about his business. 'Glad to be of help.'

Michael was given the free access to libraries, museums and other public property on any day of the week and he used his privilege. He visited the museum at the Jardin des Plantes, walked through many Paris markets and met the Professor of chemistry at the University of Paris, Professor Vanquelin, the man who discovered chromium, the hard white metal now used in stainless steel. On November 3rd 1813 Sir Humphry Davy received his Napoleonic Gold Medal at the Institut de France at a majestic ceremony. Michael continued to walk across Paris despite much snow and rain and cold.

As Christmas came near Michael had the extraordinary experience of touching history. He found himself standing on the terrace of the Tuileries Palace, Napoleon's chief residence because the Emperor Napoleon and the Empress Marie-Louise would soon pass on a state visit to the Senate. It was a long wait on a cold and wet day but at last the procession appeared. There were trumpeters and guards and officers of the Emperor and at the end of the procession Michael caught a glimpse of Napoleon wearing an ermine robe with a velvet hat plumed with feathers. Fourteen footmen were on top of the luxurious coach. Michael noticed that the crowd around him received the Emperor in absolute silence. Not a cheer was raised, no comments were made.

Two years later the man who had set out to make France a European Empire was finally defeated by allied armies commanded by the Duke of Wellington from Britain and General Blucher from Prussia at the Battle of Waterloo. Fifty-nine thousand men were killed. The man, who said 'I am the revolution' and who had conquered most of Europe by force and ruled over seventy million people, lost everything. He said he loved power like a violinist loves his violin but it all vanished. He died in lonely exile as a prisoner on the island of St. Helena in the South Atlantic Ocean.

The young Michael Faraday, looking at the passing Emperor, Napoleon Bonaparte, would die one day at Hampton Court, revered as one of the most eminent of all scientists. He would die at a home made available to him by Queen Victoria. He said in a letter to the Comte de Paris on the 7th February 1805 that he bowed 'before him who is Lord of all.'

Faraday was to bring immense benefit to the world, Napoleon Bonaparte had and would bring immense suffering and cruelty. One was to live for the Lord Jesus and the other for earthly power and glory. Two more contrasting lives never passed each other on a Parisian street.

Much to Michael's relief Sir Humphry now decided it was time to move on. The weather and his lack of knowledge of the French language had taken away any great enjoyment of Paris for Michael. His party left Paris on December 29th and travelled in extremely cold weather to the Forest of Fontainebleau. Michael was enchanted at the beauty of the land gripped by the delicate patterns of hoarfrost up to half an inch thick. After a few days they reached Lyon where Napoleon wanted Sir Humphry to study the extinct volcanoes. The beautiful Mont Blanc now rose on the horizon and Michael was delighted to see the Alps for the first time as the sun set and the moon rose. They moved on to Montpellier where they stayed for a month and Sir Humphry searched for sources of iodine by the Mediterranean Sea.

All around Montpellier the locals were preparing to fight the oncoming armies of the Duke of Wellington but Michael was not at all alarmed. He even walked past the sentinels on the ramparts of the local fort while cannons were firing! The party moved on to Nimes and Avignon, crossed the Rhone on the rope-ferry and at an inn they were even offered a bed the Pope had occupied six days previously.

Bad weather closed in and the Davy coach now turned to go up the valley of the Rhône to enter Italy. Huge icicles of frozen water were scattered on the road where the water had poured off the rocks. Michael found many of them simply impossible to lift. He was now wearing two waistcoats, two pairs of stockings under thick leather overalls and shoes. He even kept his nightcap on because it was so cold on the roof of the carriage!

'Monsieur, I must warn you,' said one of the mountain men who was to help Sir Humphry and his party over the six thousand feet high Cole de Tende, into Italy. 'There are dangerous avalanches in this area and precipices and deep invisible hollows in the snow. We have gathered over sixty men to help you over the mountain, but be careful.'

'One step at a time!' answered Sir Humphry cheerfully. 'You, Faraday, walk with me. Lady Jane and her maid will go ahead on the sedan chairs carried by the hired porters.'

The men dismantled the carriage and roped it to sledges. The sledges were then hitched to mules and driving the mules forward the whistling, shouting, cheerful men of the mountain took the Davy party under their wing. They moved at one stage, along a very dangerous ridge, but eventually reached the summit.

'Monsieur! Monsieur! I warned you,' cried the leader of the mountain men, laughing. Michael had fallen into a hollow in the snow as they made their descent and was now standing with the snow up to his chest.

They travelled on to Turin and Genoa and when they got to Lucca in Tuscany a great surprise awaited them.

'I say, Mr. Faraday!' said the carriage driver to Michael. 'I reckon the whole town is outside those famous walls.'

Michael looked ahead to the town that held some of Italy's finest medieval treasures. He could see the many splendid towers and churches of Lucca on the horizon and the driver was right, a huge crowd was milling about outside the town walls.

'Is there something wrong?' asked Michael.

'Doesn't look like it to me,' replied the driver as the town came nearer. 'I think I've just heard them cheering.'

'What for?' asked Michael.

'Us!' replied the driver as the carriage began to move past the crowds lining the road.

It was true. They had arrived one day ahead of the liberating English army and the people of the town were so relieved to be rid of Napoleon's occupying army they would have cheered the sight of an Englishman's dog not to speak of a carriage full of English people. Sir Humphry and Lady Jane waved like a conquering King and Queen and Michael sitting by the driver waved to the crowds enthusiastically grinning down upon them from his high perch. It was a very different experience to France where they could have easily been arrested as spies.

They travelled to Florence in Tuscany, the city founded by the Romans famous for the artists Leonardo da Vinci and Michel Angelo as well as Galileo the astronomer. They stayed at a grand hotel and Michael was fascinated to visit a museum of natural history with Sir Humphry.

'Faraday, look here,' said Sir Humphry. 'Here is the telescope with which Galileo discovered the moons of Jupiter in 1610.'

Michael's sense of wonder overwhelmed him.

'Look at the electrical machines,' said Michael excitedly. 'I've never seen a magnet as big as this. It says here that the magnet can lift a weight of 150 pounds.'

The scientific instruments of Florence's greatest scientists were housed at the museum and Michael found his tour of the museum was like being in Aladdin's cave.

There was a laboratory in the museum and Sir Humphry and Michael worked in it for two days on iodine. They then set out to experiment with, of all things, a diamond. They placed the diamond on a perforated dish mounted on a platinum rod inside a thick glass globe. They then filled the globe with hydrogen, which they ignited to heat the diamond. They moved the equipment into the garden, drew off the hydrogen and drew in oxygen which they had made as pure as possible. Then using the famous lens of the Duke of Tuscany they focused the sunlight onto a pinprick point on the diamond. The heat eventually rose to about 700 degrees centigrade. The diamond, the hardest substance known to man started to burn and then became a heap of black dust. They had achieved what many scientists across the world at that time thought impossible. They proved for the first time that a diamond is pure carbon. Michael had the week of his life. He was beside himself with joy at what they had achieved. He had seen iodine discovered and a diamond burnt to a pile of black dust.

Their next destination was Rome. Michael set off for a stroll through the city at the earliest opportunity. It was Easter week and he visited St. Peter's where he noted there were 2,000 huge wax candles burning in a chapel and he watched thousands of Roman Catholics from various religious societies in procession. He was amazed to observe the city erupt with gunfire at around 10 a.m. to celebrate Easter. People shot guns and pistols into the air for about two hours and Michael stood watching it all with amazement and wrote in his journal how the people took this method for expressing their joy for the Resurrection!

Michael's deepest amazement, though, came when he viewed ancient Rome. He visited the ancient Roman Forum, the Palace of the Caesars,' the baths of Trajan, the Pantheon, and was deeply impressed, even astonished by the Colosseum. As the Davy carriage passed it in the moonlight on May 7th 1813 at around 2 a.m. Michael noted it was 'beautiful in the extreme.' The Davy party left Rome at such an early hour to avoid robbers and gendarmes joined them at dawn to protect them as they passed through dangerous country.

***

'Run for your life!' cried Sir Humphry. 'The wind has changed.'

It was a week later and Michael found himself up Mount Vesuvius with Sir Humphry and a servant boy viewing the great grumbling volcano. The flames roared, lava streams broke the ground all around them and as the wind changed a huge, billowing, poisonous, suffocating cloud of smoke was blown towards them. They ran to a place of safety.

'I don't believe it!' laughed Michael as he saw the servant boy pull some eggs from his bag, crack them and then fry them on a hot stone.

'I do it often!' laughed the boy. 'They are delicious.'

They all went up the mountain the next day in order to see the volcano at night and had a glorious dinner of bread, chicken, turkey, cheese, wine, water, and of course, delicious fried eggs on-the-rocks.

They ate from cloths laid out on the smoking lava. They toasted Old England and sang heartily *God save the King* and *Rule Britannia* and a Russian sang some Russian songs.

Michael later accompanied Sir Humphry to dine with the Queen of Naples and then the party moved on to Geneva in Switzerland. On the way they met one of the greatest scientists in the world at that time, Alessandro Volta. The teenage bookbinder was now, in the hand of God, moving far from his roots and having incredible experiences. However, Lady Davy was determined that he would never forget his roots. She was downright nasty to him, in fact so nasty that Michael began to toy with the idea of leaving the whole lot of them and going home to London.

When in Geneva the Davy party stayed as guests of the Professor of chemistry at Geneva, Charles de la Rive. They stayed at his villa by Lake Geneva and the Professor began to notice what an extraordinary person Michael was. Sir Humphry went on fishing and shooting expeditions and Michael was responsible for loading his gun. Their days at Geneva however, also included continued work on iodine and experiments on the prismatic spectrum. Professor de la Rive had been carefully watching and listening to Michael.

'Faraday, would you now go down and eat with the other servants?' said Lady Davy one day when a meal was about to be served.

'Immediately,' said Michael.

'Lady Davy,' interrupted the Professor, 'I refuse to let Mr. Faraday go. In fact if you insist that he eat with the servants I will join him. I wish to share his conversation.'

'Very well Professor,' said Lady Davy, seething.

Michael decided to put up with Lady Davy's persecution because he knew that the wider reward of staying for the rest of the European tour meant a continuing improvement of his knowledge of chemistry and the sciences. His gain was worth the pain of Lady Jane Davy. The tour continued to

Germany and back to Italy, this time to Venice and back to Rome for Christmas.

When in Rome Michael visited many of the sites he had seen on his first visit, and his journal tells us, he began to search for a Bible. In all of the shops in Rome he visited he simply couldn't locate a small pocket Bible. Indeed, when he asked for one the shop assistant seemed afraid to answer. If there was a Roman Catholic priest in the shop who overheard Michael asking for a Bible, he would give Michael a very curious look.

At that time of the 19th century the Roman Catholic Church was not enthusiastic towards the idea of the Bible being available in common, everyday language. They preferred that the Bible would be kept in the mysteries of the Latin language. Why was Michael looking for a Bible? Were there spiritual longings in his heart? We do know that he was not impressed with the churches in Rome being filled at the beautiful season of Christmas with crowds of people that he had seen behaving in a most un-Christian fashion in the streets a few minutes earlier. Michael felt they were being hypocritical. Something, it seems was stirring in Michael's soul. Not that it would have been easy to spot for he was found walking with revellers on their way to a masquerade ball between 2 a.m. and 5 a.m. in the morning. He was dressed in a priest's cloak and hood with a mask, a bit like the *Phantom of the Opera*. He had just watched the cruel riderless horse race at the Piazza del Popolo. Five competing horses wearing tin plate with dangling spiked balls hurtled round the course, terrified by the howling crowd and the pain inflicted by the spikes digging into their flanks.

Michael, though, was not actually going to the masquerade but to the Accademia dei Lincei where he was to meet up with Sir Humphry to do some scientific work.

Sir Humphry had plans to move on to the famed city of Constantinople but a shattering event was to change his and most of Europe's life over the next few months. The brilliant, masterful but utterly ruthless dictator Napoleon who had abdicated as Emperor of France on April 6th 1814 had escaped from exile on the island of Elba and landed in France early in March 1815. The French people flocked to him and now he was rebuilding his army expecting to face the combined armies of Russia, Prussia, Austria, Sweden and Britain. Sir Humphry decided it was time to go home. In the meantime Michael and Sir Humphry had been working on the explosive gas chlorine dioxide which Sir Humphry had just discovered!

The great European tour was now coming to a close and crossing the Austrian Tyrol, the Davy party travelled through Austria to Germany and Belgium and eventually they rolled into the port of Ostend and embarked for Deal in Kent, England. As they entered the safe anchorage of Deal, its castle was well prepared to face any Napoleonic attack. It had first been built to defend the harbour by Henry VIII. Napoleon, though was not on Michael's mind as he saw the English shore approaching. He was just glad to be home and looked forward to seeing his family and friends. The tyrant Lady Davy would thankfully not ever get as close to him again. He was truly delighted about that.

Not Every Girl Likes a Windmill

The Battle of Waterloo was one of the most decisive battles ever fought in Europe. Fought south of Brussels at Waterloo in Belgium on June 18th 1815 it saw Bonaparte's army defeated and brought to a close twenty three years of war.

Another battle was being fought in England at that time though not with cannon or sword. It was a battle between Michael Faraday and the Librarian of the Royal Institution, William Harris and his niece.

'I've just been appointed "Assistant in the Laboratory and Mineralogical Collection and Superintendent of the Apparatus" at the Royal Institution' said Michael to his friends. 'I have been given accommodation in my old rooms at the Institution and Mr. and Miss Harris who now occupy them won't give them up.'

'Do you think they'll go in the end?' asked a friend.

'Battle is joined,' Michael joked. 'The Enemy will have to retreat!'

They did and he got his old rooms back. He now began to work with the Professor of chemistry at the Royal Institution, Professor William Brande. He helped him as his Assistant in his public lectures and amongst other duties he aided him in his experiments on coal gas. This was an area that had caused great problems in the coal-mining industry where many miners had been killed in coal gas explosions.

In 1815 the Chairman of the Society for Preventing Accidents in Coal-Mines plead with Sir Humphry Davy to try and find a way to prevent the terrible loss of life.

'Mr. Faraday, can I call on your time to help me in this problem?' asked Sir Humphry as the autumn of 1815 rolled across England.

'Are there many accidents, Sir Humphry?' asked Michael.

'Too many,' answered Sir Humphry. 'Fire damp* or methane gas deep in the coal mines explodes when it comes in contact with the miners candles which they have on their helmets to light their work. The miners cannot really tell where the methane gas lurks. The miners put small birds in cages and carry them deep into the mines. When oxygen gets low the birds quickly faint and soon die and miners know they have a very short time to escape before methane either suffocates them or explodes.'

'If we could solve that problem a lot of lives would be saved,' said Michael, enthusiastically. 'How do you think it could be done?'

'I would like to find a light which would be safe to use where methane is present that would, at the same time, consume the methane!'

---

* Fire-damp is composed of methane and other gases. It is the natural gas given off by coal in coal mines.

'What a challenge!' answered Michael with wide-eyed anticipation.

'Let's go for it Mr. Faraday,' replied the great chemist. 'Let's begin with those samples of soil we brought back from Tuscany. You remember how we experimented in Florence and how the soil gave off pure methane gas.'

It must have been heart-thumping, sweaty-palmed work as Michael and Sir Humphry Davy experimented with the Italian samples finding out just at what point the gas exploded when mixed with air. They tested the gas in foot long glass tubes as well as metal tubes. Soon they actually managed to separate the flame from the gas.

Eventually with a mixture of Michael's dextrous fingers and brain and Sir Humphry Davy's scientific knowledge and reasoning powers an amazing breakthrough was made that is now known across the world as the 'Davy Lamp.' It was safe to use anywhere in the coalmines. Coal was vital to the Industrial Revolution in Britain. Steam engines were driven by coal and Britain depended on coal to drive its industries. In 1800, for example, over ten million tonnes of coal was excavated from British mines and by 1900 that had risen to 250 million tonnes. The 'Davy Lamp' became known as 'The Miners Friend': it gave off light but a wire gauze acted as a barrier between the heat given off and any gas it might have had contact with.

It is a horrendously sad fact that in the first half of the 19th century children under five years of age worked underground for twelve hours a day and for two pennies a day. Older girls carried buckets of dry coal which were far too heavy for them and caused deformities. One woman gave birth and was expected to be back at work that very same day. She did as the Manager demanded. In one mine fifty-eight deaths out of a total of 349 in one year involved children thirteen years or younger. The breakthrough that Sir Humphry and Michael accomplished made a huge contribution to the protection of life in the mines.

'I think you should give us a lecture at the City Philosophical Society, Mr. Faraday,' said John Tatum its Director. He little knew that he was opening a door to one who would become an incredible lecturer and to a career in lecturing that still touches the 21st century. Humbly Michael rose to give a lecture on chemistry hoping his efforts would be given a favourable reception and fulfil his duties as a member of the City Philosophical Society. He warned he might fail. He certainly didn't fail.

'That's seventeen lectures you've given now, Mr. Faraday,' said John Tatum in May 1819, three years later. 'Everyone of them has been most interesting.'

'I have been greatly helped in public speaking by attending the Thursday evening classes given at the Royal Institution by the great teacher Benjamin Smart on the subject of oratory,' said Michael generously.

'Well, whatever he is teaching you, it is working, Mr. Faraday, you have become a very accomplished public lecturer. It is quite obvious that you love words and it comes across. When you combine that love of words with your knowledge of science you bring science alive.'

'I do love words, Mr. Tatum, I have already learned some parts of Shakespeare's plays by heart and some of Lord Byron's poems,' said Michael quietly.

The smartly dressed, word loving, articulate experimental scientist Michael Faraday had come a long way since the days he played on London's streets and ate at a time of crisis only a loaf of bread in a week.

Michael now began to settle down to work with Professor Brande at the Royal Institution. He was given some work to do on *The Quarterly Journal of Science* and began to write some articles himself. He helped the Professor with his experiments.

In June 1817 Michael had a holiday in Devon that he truly enjoyed. The next time we find him away from London is in July and August 1819 when he visited Wales with his friend Edward Magrath, visiting iron and steel works at Dowlais and a copper works at Swansea. He then went North to Caernarvon and Anglesey. Michael kept a journal of his journey and it tells of how he loved the landscape he journeyed through and delighted in the people he met.

'Listen to those children singing in the classroom,' said Michael one day when passing a Welsh school. He stopped in his tracks enchanted by the sound.

'It's beautiful, Michael,' said Edward.

'Never heard anything more pleasurable in my life,' said the scientist, listening. He later recorded how he was so disappointed when the children's song was finished.

'I'm really looking forward to visiting Cader Idris and the waterfall at Melinford,' said Michael. 'They tell me that this wild part of Wales is delightful.'

When they got there a little girl walked with him all the way to the Falls. She spoke only Welsh. Nevertheless, they chatted together as they walked. The little girl then ran ahead around a corner and laughed with delight when Michael rounded the corner and saw the Falls for himself. She then led him under the stream of water and gathered strawberries for him, giving him a whole handful. He wrote in his journal how he had been so moved by the kindness of the child. Many years later the great Christian writer C.S. Lewis wrote that the highest minds were those who could sympathise with a child. Mr. Faraday could certainly do that and all his life was marked by a love of children.

It was, though, for the love of a nineteen-year-old girl called Sarah Barnard that Michael Faraday was, one day, found on the road to Ramsgate. Sarah was the fifth of the nine children of Edward and Mary Barnard. Mr. Barnard with Rebecca Ermes owned one of the largest firms of silversmiths at that time in England. They supplied plates to the Royal Goldsmiths and with their top quality silver were the favourites of the British in India. Michael, unfortunately was not a firm favourite with Edward Barnard. Edward and Mary sent their daughter off to Ramsgate for a few weeks for a break to get her away from Michael's constant attentions. Michael was madly in love with Sarah but she was not so sure that she loved him as fervently.

When Michael arrived at Ramsgate he went to see Sarah as soon as possible but did not make a good start. He was out-of-sorts and said things he shouldn't have said.

'Let's go for a walk to the windmill,' said Michael.

'I'm not so sure I like windmills,' said Sarah. 'But I'll enjoy the walk.'

When they got there Michael approached the miller with determination.

'Could you show us the machinery that helps makes the flour,' Michael asked him.

'Certainly,' he replied. 'Step carefully there Madam.'

'Let me tell you,' continued the miller, 'we've had windmills in England from the 12th century. Wind power had been used to move ships along and then it was applied to grinding corn.'

'There are a lot of ropes, pulleys and lines,' said Michael.

'Indeed, sir. Notice this rod, though, this was invented by William Cubitt just a few years ago. By moving the rod we can adjust the sails of the mill according to the direction of the wind.'

The conversation continued about the chief mechanical aids of the windmill but Michael noticed that Sarah was not all that impressed. Romance did not stir in her heart at the windmill!

'Let's take a trip to Dover, Sarah,' Michael suggested during his stay at Ramsgate. 'We'll climb up to Shakespeare's cliff.'

'I'd love that, Michael,' replied Sarah, more interested in an invigorating walk by the English Channel than by the investigations of the inner workings of a corn mill.

Slowly, ever so slowly, as Michael walked and talked with Sarah she began to understand him better. She began to enjoy his conversation, his observations about the world and his joy in living. On their last evening together at Ramsgate he took her to Manston in an open carriage. By now Sarah was beginning to 'melt.' Not entirely, though, for Michael had yet to fully win her heart.

Michael continued to work hard at the Royal Institution. He analysed samples of clay from across England and wrote letters about what he was doing to the great potter Josiah Wedgewood. He did forensic work on whale oil for an insurance company. In September 1820 he began to make notes of his daily laboratory work. He was to keep up this practice for forty-two years. They have since been published in seven volumes. He was also experimenting on iron and steel with a cutler called James Stoddart. He was also trying to find crucibles strong enough to withstand the intense heat needed when metals are fused in a furnace. He was also experimenting with photography and lithography, the process of printing from a flat metal surface treated so as to repel the ink except where it is required for printing. He was working on improvements to lightning conductors, analysing gunpowder for the East India Company and investigating how to dry beef, veal, cod, pork and chickens for the British Navy. He wasted few moments in his day and laced everything with a sense of humour.

How was it going with Sarah? It was going very well for on June 12th, 1821 Michael Faraday was married to Sarah Barnard at St. Augustine's Church on Watling Street in London. Watling Street was once the Roman Road between Dover and London. St. Paul's Cathedral dwarfed the church and today only its tower stands as the Nazis bombed it in 1941 during the Second World War. Michael and Sarah who belonged to the Sandemanian Chapel near to the Cathedral would have preferred to be married there. However the law did not allow them to be married in the non-conformist Sandemanian chapel. Nowadays, of course, people can be married almost anywhere, even in diving suits under the sea!

Sarah may have been slow to fall in love with Michael but when she did, she loved him for forty years. It was a very successful marriage. It was also a marriage bonded by the love Michael and Sarah had for Jesus Christ. On July 15th 1821 Michael

Faraday made a public confession of his faith in the Lord Jesus as his Saviour and of his commitment to live the Christian life. He expressed his readiness to do whatever the Lord Jesus had commanded. The confession came as Michael applied to become a member of the Sandemanian Chapel. The Christians there required that a new candidate confessed his or her faith before the assembled church. Once Michael had publicly confessed his faith he was then required to answer questions from the elders and then from any of the members of the church. When this was over and everyone was satisfied, someone prayed, laying hands on Michael in the name of the Lord, and each one of the members of the congregation then kissed him. They literally followed the Biblical exhortation to greet one another with a holy kiss.

There are no records as to the time or place of Michael Faraday's conversion. All we know is that he first publicly declared his Christian faith that July day in 1821. His whole life was to prove how deep and genuine that faith was and how vastly it influenced his thinking not only as a human being but also as one of the greatest scientists the world has ever known.

It had been quite a year for Michael but it was to contain something that was very special. The first hint of what was to become Michael's greatest scientific discovery was on the horizon of his life. It had to do with a wire carrying an electric current. It was to be his master work.

Curious and Important

'Michael, I wonder if I could ask you to do something for me?' said his friend Richard Phillips.

'What's on your mind, Richard?' answered Michael who really appreciated his gifted friend who was a lecturer in chemistry at the London Hospital and at Sandhurst.

'There has been a lot of interest recently in the study of what electricity and magnetism do with each other' said Richard. 'It has come, as you know, from the discovery by the Danish scientist Hans Christian Øersted that the current in a wire forms a magnetic field that circles around it. That defies Newton's laws of gravity and motion!'

'Yes, it was a fine discovery, Richard,' commented Michael. 'This whole question of the strange ability of electricity to create motion has caused huge scientific interest across Europe. All kinds of research are being carried out in the field of electro-magnetism.'

'Well Michael, it is in relation to that research that I would like you to do something for me. As you know I am the editor of the scientific magazine *Annals of Philosophy* and I would like you to write a paper for the magazine summing up all the research to date.'

'That's quite a task, Richard, but it is a subject that fascinates me. Why just back in April this year, I discovered with Dr. William Wollaston, President of the Royal Society and Sir Humphry Davy the significance of their experiments in electro-magnetism. Dr. Wollaston thinks that electric current travels down a wire like a child sliding down a helter-skelter and that this current is responsible for the circular magnetic force!'

'Write it all down, Michael, write it all down,' urged Richard. 'It will make interesting reading in the magazine and stir more interest in the subject.'

As he did with all the tasks that he had to carry out, Michael Faraday set out to do a thorough job for his friend Richard Phillips. Instead of just reading the published experiments Michael decided to repeat all the experiments at his laboratory at the Royal Institution before writing them up. His paper was published anonymously in two parts in *The Annals of Philosophy* in September and October 1821 but it was not enough for Michael. He needed to go further than anything he had read or heard about electro-magnetism. He was reading, as he would have put it, the book of nature written by the finger of God and he wanted to observe how it behaved even more closely.

On September 3rd, 1821 he began work at his bench at the Royal Institution. He had realised that there really was a circular force associated with an electric current and as he worked through the day he sought to come up with a demonstration of the effect. Eventually his deeply concentrated work was interrupted by his fourteen-year -old brother-in-law George. Michael did not really like company as he was working in his laboratory but he never minded being interrupted by children. He loved children particularly because their minds were not closed like many adult minds but were open to all sorts of possibilities in the world around them. He also loved their deep sense of curiosity and wonder about the world of nature.

'Come, George, come, watch this experiment. I think something very special is going to happen here,' said Michael. He assembled a battery, a cork, some wire, some mercury, a glass jar and a silver cup. To put a complicated scientific experiment simply Michael succeeded in making a current carrying wire rotate about a magnet.

'There they go! There they go! We have succeeded at last!' cried Michael. As George looked on with awe he saw Michael Faraday literally dance around the laboratory table with glee!

'Hooray! Hooray!' cheered Michael. They had just witnessed what we now call the first electric motor – that is free motion derived from electric current and magnetism alone.

If any fourteen-year-old were to walk around the modern house they could find dozens of electric motors. There are motors in the microwave oven, the refrigerator, the telephone answering machine, the vacuum cleaner and the hairdryer. In a car there are electric motors in the power windows (a motor in each window), in the heater fans, the windshield wipers, the starter motor. Each disc drive in a computer has two or three electric motors. Today there are electric motors in swimming pools, jumbo jet aircraft, ocean going ships and even in spacecraft. Almost every mechanical movement that we see around us today is caused by an electric motor. It can all be traced back to that day in London in 1821 when Michael Faraday danced around his laboratory bench.

'Let's go to the theatre, George,' said the exultant Michael.

'Where shall we go?'

'Let's go and see the horses at Astley's,' said George.

Philip Astley had opened Astleys Amphitheatre in 1777. He was a former riding school owner and the shows at Astley's featured lots of horses. The Amphitheatre mixed circus with theatre and had a circus ring attached to a stage and exploited the circus tricks that horses could do. Philip Astley, in fact, introduced the first circus to England.

'I love Astley's' continued George. 'Especially when they have military dramas with hundreds of soldiers, horses and cannons on the huge stage.'

'Let's go, George,' said Michael, putting on his coat and leaving his laboratory behind for an evening away from his experiments. As the door shut and the laboratory went silent the world would long remember what Michael Faraday accomplished in that basement that day at the Royal Institution.

Unfortunately Michael had to face a storm of criticism following his great discovery. He decided over the following eight days to submit an article to *The Quarterly Journal of Science* detailing his research and discovery. Michael then called on Dr. Wollaston but he was out of town. Within days of the article's publication the scientific world around Michael Faraday erupted. He was charged with not acknowledging information received while assisting Sir Humphry Davy in his experiments on the subject of electro -magnetism. He was accused of concealing the theory and views of Dr. Wollaston and taking the subject while Dr. Wollaston was at work on it. He was also charged, more or less, with stealing Dr. Wollaston's thoughts without acknowledgement and then pursuing them. His whole Christian character was being called into question and Michael was, understandably, deeply hurt.

Michael's ideas were in fact very different to those of Davy and Wollaston but few of those who gossiped and criticised would have been able to understand the difference. Michael immediately stated that he wished to apologise to Dr. Wollaston for not having mentioned his theory and experiments and wrote asking to see him. Wollaston agreed and they met two or three times going over the experiments together. Michael's critics, though, rumbled on and he was accused of objectionable conduct.

The truth, though, probably lay in downright jealousy. Michael's critics did not like the idea that one so low on the social scale could be so brilliant as to upstage his seniors. The Bible says that jealousy is as cruel as the grave and that its flashes are flashes of fire. Jealousy often breaks up friendships and brings tension between colleagues. It brings bitterness and finger pointing. It is a very narrow and negative thing. While some of the leading scientists of Europe acknowledged Michael Faraday's genius, he was not honoured in his own country, as he should have been. Jesus, after all did point out that even a prophet has no honour in his own country or among his own people.

'Come on, Michael, I am behind you all the way,' said his friend Richard Phillips.

'I need your friendship more than ever, Richard,' said a very discouraged Michael. 'It is not easy to have to face such vicious criticism. It is a very lonely experience. I am doing my best to face it all head-on.'

'I will give you further space in *The Annals of Philosophy* magazine to finish your *Historical Sketch of Electro-magnetism*. I will add a final statement to what you have written in your support. Let me tell you what I am going to write: "We earnestly recommend Mr. Faraday to continue his researches on a subject which he has so ably illustrated and enriched by his discoveries that are in the highest degree curious and important."'

'A friend in need is a friend indeed,' said Michael, quietly.

While Sir Humphry Davy was still treating Michael Faraday as his servant, the world away from London was treating him as a genius. That genius during Christmas 1821 dangled a length of wire from the laboratory ceiling at the Royal Institution, electrified it and made it move under the force of the earth's magnetism alone.

'A little Christmas surprise, Sarah,' said Michael to his wife during the Christmas period. 'I want to show you the effects of electro-magnetism up to my latest stage of research.'

'Can George come too?' asked Sarah.

'Of course he can' answered Michael.

When they both reached Michael's laboratory he demonstrated to them how far his research work had reached.

'Do you see, George? Do you see?' said Michael as the wire began to revolve. Michael's eyes sparkled with enthusiasm. The fourteen-year-old George Barnard had the inside track to the heart of electro-magnetism.

Michael and Sarah Faraday were never to have any children of their own but as Michael's scientific career blossomed he never forgot the importance of children and did his best to help in their education in any way he could. He always had time for his nephews and nieces and one of them, Margery Reid, has left on record how she was allowed to sit quietly in his laboratory with her needlework. She told how her uncle would often stop his work and speak a kind word to her or even when deep into some complex experiment, would lift his head and nod to her. He would even sometimes throw a bit of potassium into water to amuse her. Often he would give Margery good advice when she had misbehaved or rebelled, showing her the importance of submitting to reproof. He would often read aloud to her, his voice breaking with emotion and tears rising in his eyes when great literature moved him.

Michael Faraday was a man of deep enthusiasms. He had outbursts of joy in his laboratory when he discovered new phenomena and he experienced great joy when reading great literature. He also expressed great joy when he was praising God at the services in his church. Such an exuberant temperament also had a dark side. He had a volatile and fiery temper. By God's grace and not without difficulty, he managed to keep his temper under control. Few people would have realised that the gentle Michael Faraday was at times seething inside particularly when he was being treated unjustly. By submitting himself to the Lord Jesus he began to display in his life the characteristic traits of a sincere Christian. In the place of pride he showed humility. In the place of anger, he showed meekness, refusing to do harm to others and displaying a deep desire for peace making. He also showed a passion for and a pursuit of God and of good. He particularly refused to lead a lifestyle of grasping and pursuing material things as an end in itself. He became well known for his care for the disadvantaged, the poor and the sick.

The significance of Michael Faraday was recognised in July 1823 when he was given the honour of being elected by the Accademia Economico-Agraria in Florence, Italy to its body of Academic Correspondents. Later that year the Institut de France gave him a similar honour. He began to apply his scientific knowledge in all sorts of interesting corners.

'Would you analyse some atmospheric air we have brought from the Arctic in glass tubes?' asked the astronomer George Fisher.

'Would you analyse sea-water and its effects on the boilers of steamships?' asked a committee seeking to improve communication between London and Dublin. Michael went even further, he advised as to the best kind of coal to use at sea.

'Would you come to Swansea and advise us on what to do with our industrial works?' asked one industrialist. 'Our eighty-four furnaces are pouring out deadly "copper smoke" into the surrounding urban area and countryside.' He was facing being in Court because it was claimed that the fallout was destroying nearly all the vegetable and animal life in the area as well as making thousands of acres of land useless.

It was the biggest industrial pollution in the nation at that time. Michael went to Swansea with his friend Richard Phillips to help.

Another great scientist now began to take Sir Humphry Davy's place in Michael's life. Davy, jealous of his brilliant servant, was the loser. Ampère, the emminent French scientist respected Michael deeply and the discoveries he had made in physics and chemistry. They wrote to each other and became great friends. Michael, who had in fact been tempted to resign from a life of scientific pursuits because of the discouragement he received in London, was now deeply encouraged to keep going through his friendship with Ampère. Today a statue of André-Marie Ampère can be found in the city of Lyon. When the Eiffel Tower was built in Paris, Ampère's name was placed on a plaque with seventy-two other prominent French citizens.

***

Michael's work though, was by no means a safe occupation.

'Michael! Michael! What have you done?' cried Sarah Faraday. It was a Saturday evening and she had rushed down to the laboratory of the Royal Institution on hearing an explosion. She found Michael with blood streaming down his face.

'Ah! Sarah! One of my glass tubes exploded while I was experimenting.'

'But Michael, this is the third violent explosion in recent days!' said Sarah picking pieces of glass off his face.

Michael had been exploring the liquefaction of gases, particularly chlorine and he was very fortunate to have escaped so lightly. Unfortunately, though, he did not escape another fire storm which now rose against him at the Royal Society. Some people felt that it was time for Michael to be recognised with a Fellowship at the Royal Society, the top gathering of scientists in Britain. Sadly a member (called at the Society a Fellow) named Henry Warburton and Sir Humphry Davy led an attempt to keep Michael out of the Royal Society. They harped back to the old controversy of Michael's article in *The Annals of Philosophy* on electro-magnetism. Then, to make matters worse, Sir Humphry Davy appears to have had some doubts as to whether the making of chlorine into a liquid was Faraday's own idea. He claimed that it had originated with him! Today chlorine is used to produce safe drinking water the world over. It is also used in the production of paper, medicine, food, paints, plastics and many other products used in every day life.

Michael read a paper to the Royal Society in March 1823 about chlorine and then published the results of his experiments, which in fact could have cost him his life. Now the deeply jealous Sir Humphry was casting doubt on whether or not Michael had, by his own work, liquefied chlorine. The truth was that he had but Sir Humphry was not going to let him enjoy his success.

'Take down that nomination form,' demanded Sir Humphry at the Royal Society Headquarters in Somerset House. He was referring to the form that put Michael forward as a candidate for election to be a member of the extremely learned society.

'I did not put it up, Sir Humphry, so I am not going to take it down,' Michael replied.

'I then demand that those who proposed you for this honour take the form down,' said the sullen, jealous scientist.

'That won't happen, Sir Humphry,' Michael said quietly. There were in fact some very distinguished scientists who were supporting Michael's nomination.

'Then I'll take it down myself,' said the irate Sir Humphry.

In his answer to this unfair and downright cruel statement Michael Faraday gave what the Bible calls 'a soft answer.' 'A soft answer turns away wrath,' the Bible teaches. What did Michael say? He said: 'I'm sure you will do what you think is good for the Royal Society, Sir Humphry.'

Michael's faith in Christ had brought out what the Bible calls one of the fruits of the Holy Spirit. It is called meekness, which is, in part, a desire for peace making. The battle to remain calm in the face of jealousy could not have been easy for Michael. For six long months his nomination ebbed and flowed. It was announced to the membership eleven times for discussion but he was finally elected on June 8th, 1824. Only one person voted against Michael's nomination and as the voting was secret it will never be known who had held out against him. It is fascinating though, to note, that the young book binder who had first arrived at the porter's desk in Somerset House to hand in a letter to Sir Joseph Banks, the President of the Royal Society asking for any kind of work, even bottle washing, had now been elevated to become one of its most prominent Fellows. Sir Joseph Banks had told the porter that Michael's letter required no answer. Michael could have given up at that stage of his life but though he did not find it easy he had pursued his interest in science with patience and dedication. 'No one from the East or the West or from the desert can exalt a man,' says the Bible 'but it is God who judges: He brings one down, He exalts another.' Michael had honoured God in his life and now God was honouring him. When God opens a door nobody can shut it and Michael went through the open door displaying very commendable grace.

Even at this important turning point in his life Michael could have been diverted. Sir Humphry Davy had turned to him and asked him to be temporary secretary at a new Gentlemen's Club in Pall Mall in London called The Athenaeum. Michael, as usual, gave his very best to the work before him, but it was keeping him away from the laboratory. When he was offered the post of Permanent Secretary to the Athenaeum, he declined and recommended his friend

Edward Magrath. Appointed Director of Laboratory at the Royal Institution in 1825 on Sir Humphry Davy's recommendation, Michael now took one of the most important steps in his life. He decided to open the laboratory and give his own lectures for Members of the Royal Institution backed up with performing his own experiments. They eventually became known as the weekly Friday Evening Discourses and arguably the most influential educational series in Britain in the 19th century.

'What an incredible mind Mr. Faraday has,' declared Maria Heimes, daughter of the Chancellor of the Exchequer, to a friend.

'Really?' asked her friend 'what kind of mind?'

'An incredibly inquisitive mind,' answered Maria.

'On a Friday evening Mr. Faraday lays out a table after his lectures that we can all go and look at. On the table are all kinds of interesting objects.'

'What kind of objects?' asked her friend.

'Oh I've seen oriental gongs, a buoyancy waistcoat, works of art, books and even a bronze of Sir Thomas Lawrence the great English portrait painter. It seems to me that anything that sparks the interest of those who love Natural History, Mr. Faraday is prepared to place, if possible, on his table. I even keep a notebook of his lectures and doodle on the inside cover!'

The tutoring that Michael had received from Benjamin Smart on oratory now showed itself in public. He had learned how to carry his listeners with him by not going too deeply into his subject while keeping to his main points. He learned not to speak too quickly but to pace his lecture. At the start he had a card placed before him with the word 'slow' written on it. Sometimes he had a card brought before him carrying the word 'time' just before his lecture hour was nearly up. Many of his listeners were sorry when he had finished. In total Michael gave 123 Friday Evening Discourses between 1827 and 1861.

In 1829 Michael's portrait was painted by H.W. Pickersgill and was engraved by Samuel Cousins. His friends and associates received copies. He was now thirty -eight years of age and had become a central figure in world science as well as a central figure in Western culture. It is a very fine portrait of Michael showing him dressed in a velvet coat and a high collared shirt. His curly hair is parted in the middle and displays his bright, enquiring eyes. He is wearing a stock, a band of white material tied like a cravat. He looks every part the gentleman that in truth he was.

'What a man that fellow Faraday is!' said a Londoner to his wife as he saw Michael pedalling down Hampstead Hill on his velocipede, an early form of bicycle propelled by working pedals on cranks fitted to the front axle. He had built the machine with his own hands.

'At least he has fun with his science!' quipped the man's wife as Michael disappeared from view. Soon multitudes of children were going to share in that fun.

A Very Special Candle at Christmas

'Ah! Mrs. Marcet, my first instructress!' said Michael enthusiastically after one of his Friday Evening Discourses. 'Never was anyone more welcome.'

'Mr. Faraday, I was never more pleased by any lecture than the one I have just heard from you. Thank you for inviting me,' replied the famous Swiss author.

'Well, Mrs. Marcet, I will never forget binding your book *Conversations in Chemistry* at Mr. Riebau's when I was a lad. Reading it introduced me to the foundations of the study of chemistry and not me only, of course, but untold thousands of other young people.'

'Well, Mr. Faraday, if they are all inspired as deeply as you what a multitude of new discoveries will be flooding the earth!'

'Thank you for coming,' said Michael. 'Remember all you have to do is mention your name at the door of the Royal Institution any Friday evening and you and a friend will be admitted immediately without a ticket. I have given orders that it be so! I hope you don't mind me sending copies of my written papers to you from time to time.'

'Not at all, Mr. Faraday, and judging by the range of topics dealt with here on Friday evenings from the manufacture of glass to Brunel's block making machine, from the ascent of Mont Blanc to the audible properties of speech, I'll be back!' Many people felt as Mrs. Marcet did and to this day The Royal Institution Friday Evening Discourses continue.

Michael now decided to introduce what would become one of his greatest legacies. In 1826 he founded the Children's Christmas Lectures at the Royal Institution. They were billed for 'juveniles,' that is boys and girls in their teen years. His goal was the same as that of his mentor Mrs. Marcet which was to communicate to children the excitement of scientific discovery. He wanted to show how wonderful it was to observe the structure and behaviour of the physical and natural world. These famous lectures were to be his great gift to children. During the next thirty-five years Michael Faraday presented nineteen of the sets of Christmas Lectures given at the Royal Institution. He gave all of the Christmas lectures between 1851 and 1861.

Michael loved to give his Christmas Lectures with a passion. It brought out the boy in him: few people in history have ever communicated the mystery and wonder of science to children as brilliantly. The Christmas Lectures still continue at the Royal Institution and many famous world scientists have given the lectures. The current Director of the Royal Institution at the time of writing is the famous TV lecturer David Attenborough.

The Christmas Lectures for Children at the Royal Institution are now televised and millions of young people over the years have watched them. Professor Carl Sagen has lectured on 'The Planets.' Professor Susan Greenfield has lectured on the 'Journey to the Centre of the Brain.' Professor Bernard Lovel has lectured on the 'Exploration of the Universe.' Karen Warwick has lectured on the 'Rise of the Robots.' Professor John Ambrose Fleming has lectured on 'Waves and Ripples in Water, Air, and Ether.' The Christmas Lectures are now the flagship of the Royal Institution.

Interestingly the Institution of Electrical Engineers founded the IEE Faraday Lecture in 1924 to commemorate the life and work of Michael Faraday. It is now billed as the United Kingdom's largest touring lecture. It is presented each year by a team of six presenters, all young people working in the engineering field. It has a tradition of presenting cutting edge technology in exciting and interactive presentations. Its aim is to interest the public and young people in particular in the world of engineering. What Michael started has become a national and international phenomenon.

Michael Faraday's lectures to teenagers were anything but boring affairs. He was well aware of the teenage boredom threshold and was not averse to throwing a coal scuttle full of coals and a poker and tongs at an electro- magnet to show the powers of magnetism as well as to keep the attention of his audience!

Perhaps his most famous set of Christmas Lectures was given on *The Chemical History of a Candle*. When it was published it soon became a classic in both scientific and children's literature. It is an astonishing piece of work. The passion Michael had for his subject is found even in the opening lines where he states that he would prefer to repeat the subject almost every year!

'There is no more open door by which you can enter into the study of natural philosophy than by considering the physical phenomena of a candle' Michael declared. He calls his audience 'My boys and girls' and states 'I claim the privilege of speaking to juveniles as a juvenile myself. I have done so on former occasions, and, if you please, I shall do so again.'

The language he uses is far from patronising; that is, he does not treat the young people before him with an apparent kindness, which betrayed a feeling of superiority. He even held up a candle that had been taken from the *Royal George* that had sunk at Spithead in August 1782, seventy-eight years previously. Though it had been subject to the action of salt water for a long period Michael stated that 'when lighted it went on burning regularly, and the tallow resumes its natural condition as soon as it is fused.'

Holding up everything from candlewood from the bogs of Ireland to delicately ornamented candles in beautiful colours, the lecturer proceeded at an absorbing pace. He describes capillary attraction showing how the flame gets hold of the fuel. Then he described to the rapt audience the philosophy of flame.

'I do not know,' he said, 'a more beautiful illustration of the philosophy of flame, as to a certain part of its history, than the game of Snapdragon.'

Snapdragon was a Victorian party game where raisins were snatched from a dish of flaming brandy. As the fascinated audience watched the little tongues of flame rising from the brandy Michael had lit from a warm dish and heard his exposition of the philosophy of flame, they were sharing the fruits of a mind that had long been informed by the power of observation.

'It is too bad that we have not got further than my game of Snapdragon,' he concluded. 'But we must not, under any circumstances, keep you beyond your time. It will be a lesson to me in future to hold you more strictly to the philosophy of the thing than to take up your time so much with these illustrations.'

'He does not need to apologise,' enthused one teenager to his friend. 'I could have listened for another couple of hours.'

'I love his illustrations,' said his friend. 'They make science much more interesting. Pity we have to wait until next Christmas for the next set of lectures. I wish I could hear him lecture to children every week in life. Wait till I get to tell my schoolteacher what I have heard tonight. I wish school was more like this!'

The Chemical History of a Candle series lasted for six lectures and though Michael Faraday did not preach Christianity in his Royal Institution Discourses and lectures he drew the series to a close with a beautiful echo of Christ's Sermon on the Mount. The Lord Jesus said that those who follow Him are 'the light of the world.' That light is derived from Him. He distinctly taught that His followers should not hide that light.

'A city on a hill cannot be hidden,' Jesus said. 'Neither do people light a lamp and put it under a bowl. Instead they put it on its stand and it gives light to everyone in the house. In the same way, let your light shine before men, that they may see your good deeds and praise your Father in Heaven.'

'All I can say to you at the end of these lectures (for we must come to an end at one time or another) is to express a wish that you may in your generation, be fit to compare to a candle' said Michael. 'That you may, like it, shine as lights to those about you; that, in all your actions, you may justify the beauty of the taper by making your deeds honourable and effectual in the discharge of your duty to your fellow-men.'

How did young people react to his lectures? Both boys and girls rushed up to his table immediately after he had finished, crowding around him. He always maintained that at his Christmas lectures he never found a child too young to understand intelligently what he had said. The effects of Michael's lecturing was perhaps best summed up in the words of Juliet Pollock in *St. Paul's Magazine* in 1870: 'his audience took fire with him, and every face was flushed.'

Another writer Mary Lloyd wrote in *Sunny Memories*, 1879, of Michael Faraday's 'touching gentleness, which, together with the brilliancy of his intellect, produced a startling effect.'

It was not long before the startling effects of Michael Faraday reached another genius who had a startling effect himself on the 19th century and who is still having an effect on the 21st. He was the great writer Charles Dickens. He wrote to Michael asking for permission to reprint one of his lectures in his magazine *Household Words*. Michael sent him some of his notes from his Christmas Lectures on the *Chemical History of a Candle*. Dickens took the story of the candle away from the young people at the Royal Institution to the fictitious Wilkinson family in London where young Master Harry asks his Uncle Bagges if he knows 'what you do when you put a candle out?' Harry has been to the Royal Institution and waxes eloquent on all he can recall from what Michael Faraday had taught him. Michael had now found a vast new audience far beyond that which crowded the Royal Institution at Albemarle Street. Dickens' series continued with such subjects as *The Mysteries of a Tea-Kettle* and *The Laboratory in the Chest*.

Perhaps his brother-in-law George Barnard, gave one of the most memorable images we have of the far reach of Michael Faraday's life. He describes how he and Michael used to go to Charles Hullmandel's conversazions. A conversazion is a scholarly social gathering held for the discussion of literature and the arts. Hullmandel was a pioneer in the art of lithography. This involved drawing images on stone that soaked them up and then the images were reproduced. Hullmandel had set up a printing shop in London to develop the whole process of lithography. Michael was deeply interested in the art of image reproduction and worked with Hullmandel on the process of lithography, which was deeply tied in to knowledge of chemistry. Michael knew how illustrations in books and on posters helped people understand science better.

Sometimes Hullmandel held one of his conversazions on board an 'eight oared cutter,' a cutter being, originally, a ship's boat, which was used for carrying light stores or passengers.

'Let's have another song, Manuel,' said Michael on one of the conversaziones on Hullmandel's cutter. Manuel Garcia, the Spanish tenor who in his lifetime wrote forty-three operas, was one of the finest opera singers of his time and a favourite in European capitals. He had been invited to sing on the cutter with his wife and daughter Maria.

'That daughter of yours will go far,' said Michael.

'You think so, Mr. Faraday?' replied her father proudly.

'Of course,' said Michael. 'Her range is limitless.'

In time Maria Garcia, later Maria Malibran became an opera legend and Chopin, Mendelssohn, Liszt and Rossini were among her staunchest fans.

'You all deserve a fine dinner after your beautiful singing,' said Michael. 'What's cooking, George?'

As the cutter made its way up the Thames Michael's brother-in-law George Barnard got cooking.

Not all Michael's life was serious study and long hours in a laboratory. He had a real zest for outdoor life. On holiday in 1824 and 1826 Michael and his wife Sarah were often to be seen taking long walks over the Isle of Wight together. Though, even on holiday, Michael did not leave all his work behind. On the Isle of Wight he wrote part of the only book of his ever published, *Chemical Manipulations,* on laboratory practice for students.

Michael Faraday had many qualities but perseverance was one of his greatest. This was the ability to continue in a course of action in spite of difficulties with little or no indication of success. For the next five years of his life Michael primarily focused on a very difficult area of science, namely the search for clear, pure glass to be used in lenses. In 1827 a furnace was built at the Royal Institution for the purpose of researching the properties of glass. It was frustrating and hard work.

Michael found it very difficult when the Admiralty got impatient with the slow progress being made on experiments being carried out for them on optical glass.

'They really are putting pressure on me, Sergeant Anderson,' Michael complained to his assistant. 'I know that the Admiralty are paying for the experiments I am doing and want results but I am not a miracle worker, Sergeant.'

'They have no idea how hard you are working on this project, Professor. I am concerned that you have developed crippling headaches.'

'To tell you the truth,' said Michael, 'I am nearing exhaustion and am thinking of resigning from the team working on optical glass. Yet I do not want to desert my post.'

'Keep at it, Professor. You may have a breakthrough sooner than you think,' said his faithful assistant. In fact he was so faithful that one night when Michael forgot to tell him to go home and let the furnace die down, he stayed all night keeping it hot. Michael discovered him still stoking the furnace the next morning!

As it turned out in the very year he thought of resigning from the team working on optical glass Michael had a breakthrough.

'It's fantastic!' said John Pond, the Astronomer Royal, talking with a friend.

'Mr. Faraday has been hugely successful in producing a seven-inch lens made at the Royal Institution furnace for an astronomical telescope. The lens transmits light without separating it into its various colours.

'What have you seen through the new telescope, John?' asked his friend.

'I have seen the Nebula of Orion, beautifully,' he enthused. 'It is one of the finest sights in the sky.'

'How far away is the Nebula of Orion?'

'1,500 light years, a light year being the time it takes light to travel in the course of one year.'

'And how far does light travel in one year?'

'About 5,850,000,000,000 miles!' said Mr. Pond.

'I do hope Michael Faraday will continue his work on lenses because he is certainly bringing outer space a lot nearer!' said his friend, smiling.

What is so fascinating about Michael's life is the wide-ranging scope of his interests. He not only loved science but, for example, as an amateur painter he loved art and enjoyed the company of artists. At Hullmandel's conversaziones he mixed in the company of Royal Academicians like the great artist J.M.W. Turner known to the world as 'The Painter of Light' and Sir Edwin Landseer the sculptor who was responsible for sculpting the huge lions still to be found in Trafalgar Square. He was even interested in the construction of musical instruments and worked on the vibration of surfaces. Samuel Wesley, the son of the great hymn writer Charles Wesley and one of the most gifted organists of the century was interested in Michael's work in vibration. Michael was the same man who in 1834 was writing on the nature of the atom!

In 1829 Michael had accepted the post of Professor of chemistry at the Royal Military Academy, Woolwich, which fortunately meant that he did not have to move away from the Royal Institution to which he was always outstandingly loyal. His new office entailed him visiting the Royal Academy weekly in term time and giving twenty-five lectures a year.

All through these years every Sunday morning and every Wednesday evening Michael would leave the Royal Institution and travel to the Sandemanian Chapel in Paul's Alley in the Barbican, London. On Wednesday evenings he would join the rest of the congregation for prayer, Bible reading and what was called public exhortation. This meant every man in the congregation was given the opportunity of speaking in order to encourage and inspire people to Christian action. Nearly all of Sunday was spent with the Sandemanian congregation singing psalms, hearing readings from the Bible and a Christian message from one of the elders. They all had a meal together called a Love Feast. The day concluded with the celebration of the Lord's Supper.

Michael, now at the very heart of the scientific community of Europe, firmly held to his belief that God spoke the physical world into existence. He believed that the world in which he experimented contained as much power as God originally introduced into the system. He believed gravitation (the movement or tendency to move towards the centre of gravity) to be at the lower end of a scale of natural powers and, usually, electricity to be at the top. He believed electricity was the highest power known to man and yet realised it was understood by few.

One of his nieces spoke of how her uncle was fascinated by thunderstorms and would stand at the window for hours watching the effects and enjoying the scene. She maintained it was for her uncle a deeply spiritual experience as he marvelled at the greatness of the Creator.

Michael held electricity in awe maintaining that its power showed the vast difference between God and humanity. He believed the structure of creation glorified the Creator. He believed that his experimental researches were aimed primarily at discovering the divinely ordained laws that governed the physical universe. He stressed the importance of improving our physical conditions through the application of science but he put greater emphasis on the role of science in improving our intellect. He was not interested in making money out of the application of his discoveries in science. He insisted that science instilled the correct moral and spiritual values. Above all Michael placed far greater emphasis on the eternal life than on the present. The present, in his story, though, was to get even more interesting as his life unfolded.

The Father of Electricity

'Captain Manby, I am delighted to welcome you to speak at the Royal Institution this evening,' said Michael with obvious delight. 'I am deeply interested in the apparatus you have invented for the saving of lives at sea.'

'Ah, Professor Faraday, it is good of you to give me a platform for my ideas. As you know, I am campaigning all around the country for a series of stations to be placed around the coasts of Britain and France where life-saving apparatus can be permanently positioned. This would mean that an immediate response could be given when ships founder offshore. You would be shocked, Professor, to learn how many seamen's lives are lost within sight of land. My apparatus will help to save lives in a storm.'

Michael Faraday was deeply interested in the sea, an interest he shared with the great painter J.M.W. Turner to whom he would talk at Hullmandel's house. Both Turner and Michael tried to encourage Manby in his work despite the fact that the Governments of Britain and France dismissed him as being a crank. Turner painted a dramatic painting of Manby's apparatus, which was shown at the Royal Academy. It had a fascinating title, which explained to the general public what was happening in his painting. It was entitled *Life-Boat and Manby Apparatus going off to a Stranded Vessel making Signal (Blue Lights) of Distress* (this painting can be viewed today on the Internet).

'Can you advise me, Professor Faraday about colour foundations in my work as an artist?' Turner asked Michael on one occasion when they met.

'I will be delighted,' replied Michael and drew from his knowledge to seek to help the great painter become an even greater one.

In 1836 Michael Faraday was appointed Scientific Advisor to Trinity House, the Lighthouse Authority which throughout its history has had as its prime objective the safety of shipping and the welfare of sailors. It was originally constituted under a Royal Charter granted by Henry VIII in 1514. Eventually Michael helped to perfect electrical lighting in lighthouses, to make the lamps more efficient and the light brighter. Even when he was seventy years old he was still to be found travelling to different lighthouses and going several miles out on the ocean to measure the brightness of the lights.

'Look, Sir Frederick,' said Michael on one occasion to Sir Frederick Arrow a member of an observer group travelling near Dover with Michael. 'Watch how I measure the luminosity of that lighthouse.'

Michael lifted a black shawl pin and used it as a photometer – as the light shone through the coloured glass of the shawl pin Michael could calculate the brightness of the size of the image.

'Why Michael, we don't really need all this elaborate equipment we brought with us after all!' said Sir Frederick, laughing.

Almost ten years to the day Michael returned to further experimentation in the field of electro-magnetism. The world was to be very glad that he did. In July 1831 he resigned from the Admiralty glass experiments handing over six volumes of manuscript notes to the Secretary of the Royal Society. He now turned back with relief to experiments with electro-magnetism that were to lead to the lighting of the cities and homes of the world. His immediate aim was to try to produce electricity from magnetism.

'Sergeant Anderson, would you please forge me a ring of soft iron in the laboratory furnace?' said Michael on Monday August 29th 1831.

'What are its dimensions to be, Professor?' asked his ever-willing assistant.

'Seven-eighth's of an inch thick and six inches in external diameter,' Michael asserted.

'It's good to see you returning to investigate electro-magnetism, Professor. Who knows just what you might discover?' said the Sergeant.

'Yes, Sergeant, who can tell where my investigation might lead?'

'At least to no more headaches, I trust,' said the caring Sergeant, hopefully.

When Sergeant Anderson had prepared the ring Michael wrapped it with two separate coils of insulated copper wire. One coil of wire was connected to a galvanic battery. The other was a continuous loop passing over a magnetic needle. Michael hoped the needle would detect any current of electricity passing through the coil. In his diary Michael noted that as soon as he hooked the first coil up to his battery he noticed a 'sensible effect' on the magnetic needle. It twitched briefly at the moment when electricity first started flowing through the coil. The same thing happened in the opposite direction as soon as the battery connection was broken. He found this extraordinary. In truth he had induced electricity in one place from electricity in another. An electric current in a coil had magnetised an iron ring and the magnetism had been deceived into making a new electrical current in another coil! He had discovered the principle of the electrical transformer.

'Good morning, driver, what a morning!' said Michael as he and Sarah settled down on their seats behind the driver on the London-Hastings coach.

'How long are you staying at Hastings, Professor Faraday?,' asked the driver as the rain emptied out of the sky.

'Three weeks,' said Michael.

'Hope it clears up for you,' said the driver with pessimism.

'I must say, Michael these newly invented Mackintoshes are wonderful protection from this awful weather,' said Sarah as they journeyed. ' What on earth are you laughing at?'

'I'm laughing at some things written in a pamphlet I am reading by my friend Richard Phillips in answer to some scientific disagreements,' said Michael.

'I think that experiment you did the other morning has put you in a good mood Michael,' said Sarah. 'Tell me, did you have to bring that iron ring and those coils of wire with you on this carriage?'

'Truth is, Sarah, I had to. I think I may be onto something big. I may turn out to be like a fisherman who sometimes pulls up a weed instead of a fish but maybe this is a very big fish indeed.'

Michael and Sarah stayed at 3, Prior Cottages, Hastings for three weeks just a few hundred yards from the sea. Michael continued to think deeply about what he had discovered and continued to prepare coils of copper and iron wire, winding them around cylinders or cones known as helices. One of the coils was 422 feet in length. He had these boxed and sent back to London.

After his holiday Michael returned full-tilt to his work. So far he had only made electricity using electricity, even if the mediator was the magnetism generated by the electricity in the first coil. As he worked on hunches he discovered on September, 25th 1831 the principle of electro-magnetic induction. Then on Monday October 17th Michael reached one of the great turning points of his life and in the history of world science. He discovered that on winding a coil round a hollow paper cylinder and connecting it to a galvanometer, electricity could be made to flow by moving a bar magnet in or out of the hollow centre of the coil. He had made the first electrical generator or dynamo. It was the first time a controlled alternating current had flown along a circuit. On that Monday morning in the great city of London the boy who had played marbles on its streets and who had been raised on the edge of poverty amongst its people had just discovered something which would bring about the end of the Age of Steam. Electricity would become a new means of locomotion. The progress of a genius had reached a new zenith. He was forty years of age.

Michael, undaunted, continued his experiments over the next five days and proved that a copper disc spinning between the poles of a magnet produced a constant current that could be picked up by terminals set at the centre and the edge of the disc. Michael had now discovered the basic principles of the production of alternating current electricity that would introduce a new age, the Age of Electricity. On the 24th November, Michael submitted a paper to the Royal Society at Somerset House summing up his momentous discoveries. Michael did not want a repeat of all the troubles he had experienced with Sir Humphry Davy and Dr. Wollaston when he had published his discoveries in *Electro-Magnetical Motions* in *The Quarterly Journal of Science* back in 1821. Sir Humphry Davy had died in Geneva in 1829 at the age of 50. Michael had been extremely generous to Sir Humphry's memory despite what he had suffered at his hand. He wrote of

Sir Humphry's 'goodness of heart' and never forgot that it was Sir Humphry who had invited him in 1812 to the Royal Institution to talk about a life of science which opened the door to his own meteoric rise to the centre of the European scientific community.

Michael had been truly Christian in his attitude to one who had at one time deeply hurt him. He had as the Lord Jesus taught, 'turned the other cheek.' However though Sir Humphry Davy had died the sting of what he and Wollaston had done remained. Michael was now making sure by depositing his paper entitled *Experimental Researches in Electricity* at Somerset House that there would be no doubt as to who had made the new scientific discoveries. His paper was placed to be read by or in front of a group of Fellows of the Royal Society. Michael and Sarah then went off to Brighton for a holiday.

Unfortunately Michael wrote to his friend J.N.P. Hachette in Paris telling him of his discoveries. This led to his letter being read out at the Institut de France and the news got into the French press. An article insisted that French Scientists had already carried out Michael's experiments. Another article by a friend wrongly maintained that two Italian scientists had discovered electro-magnetic induction first! In truth the Italian scientists had acknowledged that Michael had done so! Poor Michael got truly angry with all this. He was deeply committed to his belief that his experimental research was aimed primarily at discovering the divinely ordained laws that govern the physical universe. He wished to bring what he had discovered to as wide an audience as possible for the good of everyone.

Despite his annoyance Michael wasn't diverted from the incredible flow of creative thinking that was stirring him. He began to push what he had learned further. He wondered if electricity could be generated by using the earth itself! Was the earth a huge magnetic field?

'I wonder if the King's brother, the Duke of Sussex, could help me?' Michael asked his wife one evening.

'Whatever for, Michael?'

'Well, he is the new President of the Royal Society and I am thinking of doing some experiments at the Round Pond in Kensington Gardens.'

'The Round Pond?' said Sarah with surprise. 'What on earth are you going to do?'

'Well, actually, I am trying to see if the movement of the earth, spinning on its axis, could induce electricity in a wire running in a North-South direction. The cleanest connection to the earth is, I reckon, through water. The Round Pond in Kensington Gardens has a fine plaster bottom and is relatively free of mud. It is fed by a filtered public water supply. I need royal permission to use the pond and I think the King's brother could help me.'

'Michael, does that brain of yours ever stop working?' smiled Sarah who was as fascinated by the workings of her husband's brain as anybody in the scientific world.

The day arrived when Michael found himself in Kensington Gardens garnering the help of the garden staff of the Royal Palace. Each end of a copper wire 480 ft. long was attached to a pair of large copper plates, one at the North end and the other at the South end and sunk to the bottom of the pond. The needle of the galvanometer, the instrument which detects and measures small electric currents, did flick. There was electricity generated but Michael was convinced it was the result of what he called 'ordinary causes' and not from the earth's movement.

Two days later, Michael was found on London's Waterloo Bridge. It was morning and the tide was ebbing.

'Thomas!' said Michael excitedly to another of his assistants, Thomas Pearsall. 'I know there is nearly a thousand feet of copper wire here but it could prove useful indeed. Lower the two terminals I have brought into the river, one at the North end of the bridge and the other at the South end and see what happens. Forgive me leaving you but I do have to go back to write some letters at the Royal Institution.'

'When will you return, Professor?' asked Thomas.

'Around six thirty this evening,' said Michael.

With that Michael strode away through the crowd of extremely curious people who had gathered. Nothing like this had ever happened at Waterloo Bridge before.

By 6.30 in drizzling rain, Michael was back on Waterloo Bridge gazing down at the returning tide.

'The needle of the galvanometer is flickering, Professor Faraday,' said Thomas Pearsall. 'The electrical current is flowing the same way it was this morning.'

'My morning note says it was flowing the reverse way this morning,' said Michael tersely.

'I disagree,' said his assistant firmly.

'We will come back again tomorrow,' said Michael, as determined as ever to find scientific facts.

They returned to the bridge the next day but they did not get any positive results. Michael Faraday's theory that the earth's rotation could generate electricity was later proved by others to be correct. His work though continued to show the reach of his mind.

It must have been a relief for Michael when his paper *Experimental Researches in Electricity* was read at the Royal Society in late November 1831. It firmly established his discoveries in the area of electro-magnetism with priority being given to him as the discoverer. A further paper by Michael on terrestrial magnetic-electric induction, was read before the Royal Society on January 12th, 1832.

Michael lectured about his recent discoveries in electricity at his Friday Evening Discourses on 17th February 1832. However, a problem was raising its head. What would he call the new phenomena he was uncovering? How would he find straightforward words that the average person could use when referring to them? He knew very well that if he did not do something about it other scientists and philosophers would find some almost secret language to describe his discoveries that only they could understand.

The answer lay with his friend the Rev. William Whewell the Professor of Mineralogy at Cambridge University, later Professor of Moral Philosophy, Master of Trinity College and eventually Vice-Chancellor of Cambridge University. Professor Whewell believed that the laws of science are evidence of the existence of God and that the discovery of these laws was a task that had been given by God in order to bring humankind to a greater understanding of the majesty of His design. Michael wrote to Professor Whewell to ask for help in creating a new language of electricity. They went back to ancient Greek for their inspiration. The letters that passed between them on the meaning of Greek words gave Michael an education in itself. When Michael would have ideas for words for his discoveries he would send them to Professor Whewell and usually by return of post he'd get a suggestion. So the world got such words as 'anode,' 'cathode,' 'ion,' 'diamagnetic,' 'paramagnetic,' 'electrolyte,' 'electrodes' and 'electrolysis.'

It was a measure of Michael's status in the nation when in June 1832 he received an Honorary Degree of Doctor of Civil Law at Oxford University.

'That chap Faraday is a Dissenter, you know. He is not a member of the Church of England,' said an onlooker at the ceremony.

'I know,' replied the person sitting beside him. 'You can't even be admitted as a student to Oxford University without professing to be a member of the Church of England. Faraday would not even have been admitted here as a student! This honour is an almost unheard of distinction for a working class lad and a Dissenter.'

'He must be special,' said the onlooker. 'They say he is England's greatest natural philosopher.'

He certainly was and while it certainly took far more than Michael's genius to forge the Electrical Age he was most certainly the father of it.

Perhaps the mother of it as far as the average person was concerned was a close and deeply respected scientist friend of Michael's called Mary Somerville. Michael kept two lithographs of Mary in his album of portraits of his colleagues and friends. Mary, a fair-haired, grey-eyed Scot, was one of the most remarkable women in Europe. Today she is remembered by a famous College, which bears her name in Oxford University. Somerville Hall, later Somerville College, was founded in 1879 to provide an opportunity for women who at that date were excluded from membership of the University to gain some kind of higher education in Oxford. Somerville College has been attended by such outstanding women as Indira Gandhi who became Prime Minister of India and Margaret Thatcher, who became Prime Minister of the United Kingdom. The College though was particularly connected to science and in 1964 another Somerville College graduate, Dorothy Hodgekin was awarded the Nobel Prize for Chemistry. A long and distinguished line of writers have also come from the College. Mary Somerville, a top class mathematician was famous for her books particularly the *Mechanism of the Heavens*. Her books helped the average person understand science.

'Will you look over the proofs of my book *On The Connexions of the Physical Sciences* Michael?' ventured Mary one evening as Michael visited her home with other scientific friends in London's Hanover Square. (Connexions was the 19th Century spelling of the word 'connections'!)

'It will be a pleasure, Mary,' replied Michael. 'I greatly support your writing because it will help to educate the masses in the understanding of science.'

'Thank you, Michael. I would particularly like you to look carefully at what I have written on electricity and magnetism. Nobody knows more about the relationship between those two than you do.'

'I like your painting too, Mary,' said Michael, looking at one of Mary's works on her wall.

'It's a start,' replied Mary. 'But I'm afraid it's far from the standard reached by our mutual friend Mr. Turner.'

'Ah! Mr. Turner,' said Michael with affection. 'I love the story of the lady, who said, "I don't understand your paintings, Mr Turner." To which Mr. Turner replied, "Don't you wish you could, Ma'am, don't you wish you could!"'

Mary Somerville and her husband attended Michael's Discourses regularly. The objects in the

Somerville's Rooms at Hanover Square were not unlike those that sat on Michael's famous table following the Friday Evening Discourses at the Royal Institution. There were crystal models here and shells there and fossils yonder. There was a telescope in a case, over there were bows and arrows of interest and of course, Mary's easel. Apart from all her scientific work Mary also had five children to raise. Today Somerville College houses some of Mary Somerville's own paintings. She was one of Michael Faraday's best-loved colleagues. She died in Naples, Italy in 1872 at the age of ninety-one.

Not everybody, of course, was on Michael Faraday's side during these great years of discovery. He was regularly criticised by a teacher of science at the East India Company College called Thomas Sturgeon. Sturgeon thundered against Michael in his magazine called *Annals of Electricity* casting doubt on his theories of electro-magnetic induction. He also criticised Michael for what he called his aloof way of doing his work. Another matter arose in the 1830's that unfortunately brought Michael undeserved criticism. It began with well-meaning friends.

'Prime Minister,' said the Lord of the Admiralty, Lord Ashley to Sir Robert Peel at the Palace of Westminster. 'I wonder could I have a word in your ear?'

'Certainly, my Lord,' said the busy Prime Minister.

'It concerns Professor Michael Faraday, now Fullerton Professor of chemistry at the Royal

Institution and the Professor of chemistry at the Royal Academy, Woolwich.'

'Ah, the Father of Electricity, my Lord.'

'Indeed, Prime Minister.'

'What can I do for you, Lord Ashley?'

'On behalf of some of his friends, we would like the nation to honour Professor Faraday with a civil list pension in recognition of his outstanding contribution to science. We would like his name to be submitted to the King for this purpose.'

'Collate the facts on his life, my Lord and I will see what I can do.'

Unfortunately the Government of Sir Robert Peel lost the General Election of 1835 and a new Government under Lord Melbourne came into office. When Michael heard of what was going on his view of the matter was that he could not accept a pension whilst he was able to work for a living. That summer he went on a walking sightseeing holiday in Germany and Switzerland in the company of his brother-in-law George Barnard. The beauty of Switzerland, though, was left far behind when Michael was summoned on October 26th to No. 10 Downing Street to see the Prime Minister. First he was introduced to the Prime Minister's Secretary Thomas Young.

'I take it that my time with the Prime Minister this morning is about this pension business' said Michael.

'Indeed it is, Professor Faraday,' said the Secretary.

'I have serious objections to it, you know,' protested Michael explaining how he preferred not to lay up his wealth on earth. Michael was fully committed to laying up his wealth in Heaven. We can be almost sure that Thomas Young never had such a conversation before at Downing Street and would not be likely to ever have it again! Michael was quite clear that he would not accept the pension. He was then ushered into the Prime Minister's office. Their conversation lasted for only a couple of minutes. Michael set down a transcript of what they had said. (Today it can be found in the Institute of Electrical Engineers archive 2/3/18/9):

Mr. F. – I am here my Lord by your desire. Am I to understand that it is on the business, which I have partially discussed with Mr. Young?

Lord M –You mean the pension don't you?

Mr. F. –Yes, my Lord.

Lord M – Yes, you mean the pension and I mean the pension too. I hate the name of the pension. I look upon the whole system of giving pensions to literary and scientific persons as a piece of gross humbug. It was not done for any good purpose and never ought to have been done. It is a gross humbug from beginning to end. It...

Mr. F. rising and making a bow – After all this my Lord, I perceive that my business with your Lordship is ended – I wish you a good morning.

Michael was indignant at what had just been said. After all, he had not raised the subject of a pension.

His friends had raised it and he had been asked to go to Downing Street. When some of his friends got wind of what was happening they went into action to try and reconcile the Prime Minister and Michael. Two women in particular were at the heart of this called Caroline and Mary Fox, Mary being the daughter of King William IV. Eventually a letter came from the Prime Minister which was a virtual apology asking Michael to reconsider his decision. Michael replied immediately saying he would accept the Prime Minister's offer 'with pleasure and with pride.'

Sadly the press got a hold of what was going on and the whole story burst into the columns of *The Times*. When Michael was accused of having given details of his conversation with the Prime Minister to a magazine Michael wrote in fury to *The Times*, categorically denying it. The Royal Command for Michael's Civil List pension was given the day after Michael's letter was published.

'Don't talk to my mother about the Honours I receive, Sarah, please,' Michael pleaded with his wife.

'Why?' she answered with surprise.

'Because she is so proud of me already any more talk of my Honours will be bad for her!' laughed Michael.

He was right. Michael had supported his mother financially when she could no longer take in lodgers to pay her way. She understood very clearly that in Michael she had an extraordinarily gifted son.

If you were to look at a map of Westmoreland, England as it was in the year 1770, near the River Eden in an area known as Stainmoor Forest is marked 'Black Scar Farm.' The farm is no longer to be found in the 21st Century, but it gained its name from something we still use today. The brook that runs next to it had a bedrock of coal – hence the name 'Black Scar.'

It was on this farm that her parents Michael and Betty Hastwell had raised Michael's mother. She was their sixth child. It is highly unlikely that Michael's mother could ever have realised that her son would one-day transform the use of that coal to drive the turbines that would produce electricity to light the cities and homes of the world. Such is the romance of the story of the one Margaret Faraday called 'My Michael!' She had raised him to know and love the Lord Jesus of whom she was a faithful follower. She died in March 1838 and Michael, as the book of Proverbs Chapter 31 so wisely puts it, arose and called her 'blessed.' Margaret Faraday had entered into her eternal reward.

Reaching for the Stars

'What a night!' said a Friday Night Discourse enthusiast as he headed home on the night of January 31st 1839. 'What more will Professor Faraday show us this year?'

'I agree. Mr. William Henry Fox Talbot's photogenic drawings were amazing,' said the enthusiast's wife. 'I got quite close to them on Professor Faraday's table. I find them absolutely enthralling.'

What they were discussing, of course, was the new phenomenon of photography. Michael Faraday had given that evening the very first announcement of photography in England. Although Fox Talbot did not invent photography he discovered the process that has underpinned most photography for the last century and more. He is known as the Father of Photography. His photographic experiments culminated in his greatest achievement when he invented the positive/ negative process in photography. On 23rd September 1840 with elation and wonder he watched a picture gradually appearing on a blank sheet of paper. All images printed today in magazines, newspapers, journals and books or on posters go back to his discovery. All printed circuit boards on today's computers are miniaturised by the process that goes back to Talbot's work. Artists at the time even actually felt that their art was threatened by what he had discovered.

Photography is, of course, deeply tied to chemistry. Michael Faraday later became one of the most photographed public figures in England and was very enthusiastic about the whole subject of photography. The Father of Electricity and the Father of Photography were well matched.

'I don't feel too well, Sarah,' a dizzy Michael Faraday admitted one day in November 1839 at the Royal Institution.

'What's wrong, dear?,' asked his wife anxiously.

'I have a sensation of whirling and loss of balance and I have been suffering severe headaches' answered Michael.

'Come, lie down,' said Sarah leading Michael to a couch. 'I'll ask Dr. Latham to come and see you.'

'That would be good Sarah,' said Michael. 'I really do not feel well.'

When Michael's doctor had examined him he was quite concerned with Michael's state of health.

'Professor Faraday I am sorry to have to say this but I am going to have to order you to cancel all your future engagements and invitations.'

'To tell you the truth, Dr. Latham, I confess that I am actually dreadfully overworked at the moment,' admitted Michael. 'My whole research and thinking into the subject of electricity has not been easy work by any means and in fact, it has been very difficult to understand. I have been lecturing a lot and people are constantly consulting me on all kinds of subjects.'

'Well, Professor, you are going to have to rest from it all for awhile,' said Dr. Latham.

In all it turned out to be a two-year rest. Michael began to scale down his work at the Royal Institution and to pull away from all scientific research. He was actually suffering from acute depression of which his dizziness (called vertigo) and headaches were but symptoms. His memory was very poor.

'Listen to your friend the Swiss Professor, Michael,' urged Sarah. 'Professor Schoenbein says the Swiss Alps will do you good. I know that Brighton is very good for you but I think a good long visit to Switzerland would be even better.'

'Ah, to see Mont Blanc, again,' said Michael with rising excitement. ' How does Lord Byron put it?:

Mount Blanc is the Monarch of mountains;
They crowned him long ago,
On a throne of rocks, in a robe of clouds
With a diadem of snow'

'Well then Michael, let's do something about it,' urged a plucky Sarah.

They did just that. Apart from holidays not only in Brighton but also in Deal, Hastings, Folkestone, Eastbourne, Walmer and Margate in 1841 Michael,

Sarah, and George and Emma Barnard spent three months in Germany and Switzerland. It was a deeply refreshing time for Michael that was spent far away from the poisonous substances of his laboratory.

'I want to walk over the Gemmi Pass and back,' Michael declared one morning in his hotel room in Leukerbad, the Swiss spa town, nestling in the South Western Canton of Valais. Ten and a half hours later he was back at the hotel having walked forty-five miles through heavy rain and winds. The only affects following his journey was a little stiffness and a small blister.

While Michael revelled in the scenery, his brother-in-law George Barnard sketched it. While Michael scanned the glaciers through his telescope, George was gathering material for his paintings that would later be hung at the Royal Academy. George would also write books on the subject of landscape painting. Michael also saw an avalanche at a distance during his stay in Switzerland and was mesmerised by its irresistible force.

In October 1840 Michael had become an Elder in his local church. His duties included comforting the sick, the dying and the bereaved. He was expected to give regular exhortations on themes taken from the Bible. Comments published in W. Gerald's book, *Michael Faraday: Man of Science*, London 1891 from three people who heard Michael preach gives an idea of his style. 'He read,' said one listener, 'a long portion of the Gospels slowly, reverently, and with such an intelligent and sympathising appreciation of the meaning that I thought I had never heard before.' Another noted the 'devotedness of his manner' and a third was greatly impressed by 'the amazing sense of power and beauty of the whole filled one's thoughts at the close of the discourse.'

'What are you going to preach on today Uncle Michael?' asked his niece Caroline Reid as she walked to church along Sackford Lane in the tiny village of Old Buckenham in Norfolk with her uncle and aunt. Michael's London church took some responsibility for the congregation in Old Buckenham as well as at Newcastle and Dundee.

'I'm going to speak later this afternoon on Romans 15:13,' replied her uncle. 'It says "May the God of hope fill you with all joy and peace as you trust in Him so that you may overflow with hope by the power of the Holy Spirit".'

'What a beautiful text you spoke from today Professor Faraday,' said John Loveday as he welcomed the Faradays and Caroline to his home for tea by the village green. 'We shall sorely miss you when you leave us tomorrow for London. We truly wish you lived here, Professor.'

'It's been a pleasure to visit you all, Mr. Loveday. I don't mind at all when the train leaves London for Norfolk.'

Michael was deeply loved and respected by the congregation at Old Buckenham and he, one of the most eminent scientists in Europe, deeply loved them. Many of these people were poor in material terms but Michael had been poor himself and made no difference with them. Michael also visited the congregation in Glasgow and Edinburgh.

The love shown to Michael in Old Buckenham, sadly, was not always shown to him by the London congregation. In March 1844 he was stripped of his Eldership over some point of view he held with which the leadership disagreed. Some have suggested it was because he had been commanded to have lunch with Queen Victoria on a Sunday and had attended her at Buckingham Palace rather than going to church. There is, in fact, no verifiable evidence for this. The fact that eighteen other members of his church were also excluded at this time including close friends and relatives, in all some twenty percent of the membership of his London church, shows that there was a strong feeling of unity against the church leadership's point of view. There is evidence in the wider Sandemanian denomination at that time of deep disagreements as to whether it was lawful for church Elders to make decisions without involving the whole church in their decisions.

Whatever the issue, the whole episode caused Michael Faraday deep pain and huge stress. It all came, of course on top of his problem with depression. It crippled his spirit and brought him deep heartache. Michael was readmitted to the church about one month later. He was not re-elected to the Eldership for a further sixteen years. Sadly exclusions and divisions within the Sandemanian denomination, a form of Presbyterian Church which had split with the Church of Scotland, were frequent.

There was, though, one particular person who encouraged and cheered Michael up at this difficult time of pressure and turmoil. Interestingly it was the daughter of the deeply controversial but hugely gifted poet Lord Byron. Ada, Lady Lovelace was a brilliant mathematician and she held Michael Faraday in extremely high regard. She wrote letters to Michael praising his 'moral and religious feelings' and asking him about his faith. He wrote back telling her that his hope was founded 'on the faith that is in Christ.' He maintained to her that the natural works of God always glorify Him.

'I think I see in you a man who never attempts "to serve two Masters"' wrote Lady Lovelace. '... a being who is ever willing to serve man as under God, but not to serve man instead of God, or to make man the go-between interposed between you and the Creator. And when I behold these characteristics united with high intellectual endowments I cannot but look on you then as one of the few whom it is an honour and a privilege to know on this earth.'

***

Despite his illness Michael continued to be deeply involved in his work on improving the lighting systems of lighthouses.

'The problem is that the glass in front of the lamps ices up severely in winter, Professor Faraday,' said George Neale, the keeper of St. Catherine's Light on the Isle of White as Michael arrived to inspect the lighthouse. 'There is also condensation coming from the lamps and rising from the lighthouse tower itself. This all dims the light,' explained the keeper in exasperation.

'Well as you know, Mr. Neale, I designed the chimney here at the lighthouse to carry away the smoke and moisture produced by the Argand lamps. I want to improve its efficiency.'

'What effect has Professor Faraday's visit had on your work, George?' asked a friend a few months after Michael had visited the lighthouse.

'A huge effect,' answered the lighthouse keeper. 'He made recommendations for improving the chimney, the lamps and even the arrangement of the doors in the tower. The result has been that no damp condenses on the lighthouse windows and no dirt shades the lantern. The lantern is, in fact, twenty times cleaner.'

Michael's helpful advice also continued to be felt across the nation.

'Ninety-five men and boys have been killed at Haswell Colliery in County Durham,' Michael sadly informed Sarah his wife one morning.

'The Prime Minister, Sir Robert Peel has asked me to be part of an inspection of the mines.'

'Why do you think it happened Michael?' asked Sarah.

'We will see Sarah,' answered Michael thoughtfully. 'I will go down the mine and I will have to cross-examine the witnesses of the explosion in the enquiry.'

'Please be careful, Michael,' said Sarah.

'I will,' he replied. 'Mines are truly dangerous places especially since coal production has risen and mines have become deeper.'

Michael went to inspect the mines and narrowly avoided injury in a rock fall. During the inspection he sat down on a bag of gunpowder. Suddenly he sprang to his feet.

'Put that candle out immediately,' he shouted to a man nearby. 'How can you possibly be so careless? Have you no sense? You could have had us all killed! This carelessness is what is wrong with this place. I have heard that some of you miners expose the flame of your Davy Lamps to get a better light while down the mine and even light your pipes with the flame. That can ignite gas in the mine and cause horrendous explosions.'

Michael cross-examined the witnesses of the explosion with great skill. Later he made widespread recommendations regarding safety in mines and the education of miners in aspects of chemistry and geology and procedures at work. The inquest returned verdicts of accidental death.

Those who visited Michael's laboratory at this time noticed that there were fewer tubes and retorts on his bench and fewer smells of gases in the air.

'Why, Michael this place looks much less dangerous than in past years,' quipped his brother-in-law George Barnard. 'I reckon there is less chance of being blown apart than of recent times.'

'It's true, George,' answered Michael.

'What are all these chunky prisms and magnets and batteries for Michael?' asked George. 'I've never seen so much glass on your desk before. What are you really up to?'

'I'm interested in the effects of magnetism and electricity on light,' he answered. 'Do you see this piece of heavy glass? It's actually two inches by one and a half inches and half an inch thick. I've been experimenting with it and found that when contrary magnetic poles were placed on the same side there was an effect produced on the polarised ray. I've proved that magnetic force and light have relation to each other. It led me to arrange for this rather large electro-magnet to be brought by road from the military academy at Woolwich. This electro-magnet actually holds, when in action, a half hundredweight at each end of the core! I excite this electro-magnet with five pairs of Grove's battery.'

'And what about the effects of electricity on light, Michael?' asked George, now deeply interested in what his brother-in-law was explaining.

'I found that light travels through a particular angle depending on the strength of the magnet and the direction of the electrical current. I've actually even been trying to find out if the opposite happens. Can light electrify or magnetise something? Can the sun for example generate electricity?'

'Have you found out the answer?'

'Sadly no George,' replied Michael. 'I took my equipment outdoors on a sunny morning and did my best to try to find the answer.' It would, in fact, take scientists of later years to discover the process of photo-electricity.

'I hope you are going to talk about all this in public, Michael. We really have not heard you as often in public as we would all like to.'

On Friday April 3rd 1846 Michael Faraday outlined at the Royal Institution what is now known as the electromagnetic Theory of Light. In fact the whole area that Michael was now investigating began to lead him to probe with his mind into outer space. In November 1845 he had coined the phrase 'magnetic field' at his laboratory. He was indicating how far the physical influence of a magnet could stretch. A few days following his latest lecture at the Royal Institution he penned the lecture for *The Philosophical Magazine* under the title *Thoughts on Ray Vibrations*. He wrote of light travelling through space about 190,000 miles per second, something he knew the average person would find very difficult to understand. Yet he knew he could show it was true.

Today the vastness of space is more real to us through the actual journeys of spacecraft like *Voyager* and *Galileo*. However not since Galileo himself turned his telescope towards the heavens in 1610 has any event so changed our understanding of the Universe as the deployment of the Hubble Space Telescope in 1990. Since then it has been orbiting 380 miles above the earth at five miles a second. It is the size of a school bus and weighs more than twelve tons. It helps us study the universe and planets outside our solar system, providing the deepest views of space. The pictures it sends back of deep space are awesome.

In 1858 Michael was writing about the possibility of converting the force of gravity into electricity. He saw this as motive energy for travel above the earth's surface. The young man who had ridden across hundreds of miles of Europe on the top of a horse drawn carriage often gazing at the stars was now reaching for them.

Nothing is too Wonderful to be True

'I always find that a trip to hear Professor Faraday on a Friday night at the Royal Institution does me good,' said Mary Anne Evans. She was the author of some of the most famous novels in the English language. Among them are *Adam Bede*, *Mill on the Floss*, *Middlemarch*, *Silas Mariner* and *Daniel Deronda*. In modern times some of these novels have been turned into widely viewed television series. Her pen name was 'George Eliot.'

'Why do you like him, Mary Anne?' said the editor of the prestigious *Westminster Review*, Henry Lewes, of which Mary Anne was the Assistant Editor.

'Because Henry, Professor Faraday is so downright enthusiastic. The lecture I heard recently was about the relation between nitrogen and oxygen. He showed how these gases when carried in soap bubbles behave differently when floated into a magnetic field. He told us we little knew how many hours he had spent in blowing little minute soap bubbles.'

'An incredible gentleman, Mary Anne!'

'True, Henry,' she said smiling. 'But it is his sheer enthusiasm for science that bowls me over. It is as fresh as the enthusiasm of a child.'

Michael at this time was suffering from all kinds of ailments: he had memory loss, headaches, and bouts of giddiness, deafness, quinsy, flu, chills, neuralgia, and dental trouble. He was amazingly cheerful about it all but it did effect his lecturing schedule at the Royal Institution. The fact of his being absent from the Royal Institution for prolonged periods only made his audiences want to hear more from him. He got the highest recorded audience of his life when on the 11th April, 1851, one thousand and twenty eight people crammed into the Royal Institution Lecture Theatre to hear him.

Another matter of huge public interest now began to crowd in on Michael. In 1853 people all over the country were filled with a desire to try to communicate with the dead. A lot of people had died in the preceding decade from cholera epidemics and people in the next one were seeking to find out what lay beyond death. Unfortunately they looked in the wrong place. They went to mediums who were individuals who claimed to be able to communicate between the dead and the living, a practice firmly condemned in the Bible. The reports were that when these people stood around a table with a medium the table moved in response to their questions. The practice became a craze. Michael was constantly pestered to give his view on the matter. He eventually responded under controlled conditions at the home of the Rev. John Barton, a scientific colleague and Secretary to the Royal Institution.

Michael made up a bundle of every kind of material he could think of that might transmit or prevent whatever forces might make a table turn.

'My, Professor Faraday,' said the Rev. Barlow. 'You have quite a collection here. Let's see, here is cardboard, millboard, glue, sandpaper, glass, plastic clay, tinfoil, vulcanised caoutchouc, resinous cement, and wood!'

'Well, John, let's see what happens when the materials are placed under the hands of one or more of these participants and let's see what happens when they are taken away,' said Michael.

Michael discovered that the materials made no difference to the way the table moved.

'Hand me that sheet of cardboard,' asked Michael. 'I want to fix this lightweight lever to it.'

Michael then told the group of people around the table to look at his lever while pressing downwards on the table.

'Look,' he said. 'It does not move. Now look away from the lever while pressing downward everyone.' The table moved.

Later Michael wrote a letter to *The Times* and gave his views on the matter stating that the cause of the table's movement was a seemingly involuntary muscular action. He even blamed the system of education in the country that left people open to such a 'mental condition' that caused them to be carried away by such a phenomenon.

It all proved that Michael had become the leading and most public scientist of the age. He was becoming his nation's conscience. He also proved to be something more than that. He now turned to try to improve the educational standards of his nation. The Royal Institution set up a series of lectures by outstanding scientists on how children and adults should be taught. Michael gave a lecture in the series entitled *On Mental Education*. He tore into the whole table-turning phenomenon and the lecture was the nearest thing to a sermon he ever gave at the Royal Institution.

In the presence of Queen Victoria's consort, Prince Albert, Michael declared the book of nature as being written by the finger of God. He spoke of the training of the mind as being so wonderful there was nothing to compare with it elsewhere in creation. The trained mind helped, he believed, self control.

'I believe some (scientific men) hesitate because they do not like to have their thoughts disturbed,' said Michael. 'When Davy discovered potassium, it annoyed persons who had just made their view of chemical science perfect; and when I discovered the magento-electric spark, distaste of like kind was felt towards it, even in high places. Still science must proceed ... It cannot, I think, for a moment, be supposed that we are to go no further in the investigation (of the conservation of Force). What would our knowledge of light, or magnetism, or the voltaic current have been under such a restraint of the mind?'

Despite his ailments Michael started to mix with people in public a lot more frequently during the

1850's. Somewhat reclusive socially in the 1830's and 40's Michael now began to attend, for example, Royal Academy Annual Dinners. He also dined with senior statesmen and took up a theatre box lent to him and his wife by Angela Coutts the banking heiress. He just loved pantomime as he had a huge empathy with children. He was also a shrewd theatre critic.

Michael was called upon in the middle of the 1850's to give his opinion on what design of cable would be best for submarine use. A system was being thought out to lay a telegraph cable under the Atlantic Ocean linking the Old World with the New World. The first cable was laid in 1858 and to the thrill of millions of people messages were flashed from Europe to America. Michael was also called in to help advise on how to protect paintings in the National Gallery. The air of London was sulphurous and he was asked to advise on the problem of the cleaning of pictures on public display. He also became a member of the National Gallery Site Commission that looked at various sites for the new National Gallery. The Commission sat for twenty-six days in 1857. During the sitting Michael even cross-examined England's greatest art critic and the man reckoned to be the greatest Victorian bar Victoria herself, John Ruskin.

'I think, Victoria, that we should offer Professor Faraday and his wife Sarah a grace-and-favour house at Hampton Court,' suggested Prince Albert to his wife at Buckingham Palace. 'The man has made an enormous contribution to science within his lifetime. I shall never forget the lecture he gave on mental education and his views on the whole table-turning phenomenon. He talks such a lot of sense and I love the fact that he believes that nothing is too wonderful to be true! I hear he and his wife do not enjoy good health. It would be great for them to be able to end their days on earth in the quiet surroundings of the Hampton Court area.'

'A capital idea, Albert,' replied the Queen. 'I too respect the man greatly. It is amazing that a child from such poor circumstances should rise to become a man of such great prominence. I will command that he and his wife be given the Georgian grace-and-favour house on the Green at Hampton Court for the rest of their lives.'

A grace-and-favour house refers to a house or apartment that is provided rent-free by Royal permission. Michael and Sarah were delighted to accept the offer but when Michael saw that the house was in a bad state of repair he was worried about the cost of making renovations. He need not have worried because when Queen Victoria heard of his concern she paid for the necessary renovations. The house became theirs in June 1858 and it was much loved by them. It did not immediately become their retirement residence because Michael had not yet retired but they just loved to escape there to get away from the smoke of London. Michael even wrote a poem about how he felt:

'Fair Hampton Court! what pleasant hours
Have sped beneath thy fragrant Bowers
And sweet to memory are the times
We lingered near thy shadowy limes.

And while life lasts will love be there
To those who bade us freely share
In royal gift, in fair retreat,
And more than all in friendship sweet!'

Just after his 70th birthday in October 1861, Michael tendered his resignation to the Managers of the Royal Institution. They only accepted his resignation as a lecturer to young people and Michael continued to work at the Royal Institution. However, by June 1862 he knew that it was definitely time to go. On the 20th June he rose for the last time to lecture at a Friday Night Discourse. He had an audience of over 800 people. He knew it was his last time and had carefully prepared notes to help him state that though he had spent years of happiness at the Royal Institution, it was time to leave. He particularly emphasised that it was memory loss that was causing him to be filled with hesitation and uncertainty. It was, as Michael put it, 'inability to draw upon the mind for the treasures of knowledge it has previously received.' He knew he could not reach the former high standard he had set for himself, a standard his audiences had deeply appreciated.

'It was one of the saddest things I have ever seen,' said an observer to his friend at the end of the Discourse. 'When Professor Faraday fumbled and accidentally burnt his notes this evening, I could have cried. I have listened to that man right across the thirty six years he has been lecturing here and it is heart breaking to see him come to an end of it all in such a manner.'

'We shall never see his like again,' said his friend, who had also been deeply touched by the final lecture of the great scientist at the Royal Institution. A very special era in the history of science was drawing to a close.

In November 1862, though, Michael rose to meet a challenge that was near to his heart. He was asked to give evidence before the Public Schools Commission under the Chairmanship of the Earl of Clarendon. He passionately wanted to speak on the subject of the education of young people in science. Michael began by deploring the fact that so much advance had been made in science across the past fifty years and that no attempt had been made to teach that advance to young people.

Michael believed that the lack of general scientific knowledge and its intelligent application was at the root of the educational problems facing Britain. He pointed out that the first problem to be overcome was the shortage of teachers.

'That fellow Faraday was furious today,' said Lord Clarendon to his wife when the day's work was over.

'Why?' she asked.

'Because when I pointed out that Eton School was a typical example of the kind of school I was concerned with and the 'upper classes' as the group that I was concentrating upon, Faraday informed me that he had expected I would be talking about the education of all classes of children. That fellow, you know was basically educated on the streets of London!'

'How did you answer him, my Lord?' asked his wife.

'I said that the Public School Commission was concerned with nine schools only and I listed some of them – Eton, Harrow, Winchester, Rugby, and Charterhouse.'

'And was he truly annoyed, my Lord?'

'He certainly was! He was infuriated! He came back at me claiming that adults who had been educated in public schools were ignorant of their ignorance!'

'What did he think should be taught?' asked Lady Clarendon.

'He would not give a list of his preferred sciences but he did say that he was keen on the value of teaching Greek as the root language for science. He thought a little astronomy should be taught and that chemistry ought to be taught early in a child's education. He did, though, bang on about how things like the table-turning craze showed up the fact that there was something wrong in our education system.'

'Getting a little above his station, don't you think, my Lord?' said Lady Clarendon.

'True, my dear but I have to admit he is a formidable opponent and extremely intelligent.'

Michael Faraday's appearance before the Public Schools Commission showed that despite his long association with some of the greatest minds in Britain and Europe he had not grown arrogant. Through his rise to great prominence in his nation he had not forgotten the needs of those growing up far from the wealth of the privileged classes. He had not forgotten the place where he had grown up himself.

Michael's Christian faith had protected him from being corrupted by fame and celebrity. His last great public appearance showed that his love of children was undiminished and that his deep desire that they be better educated was one of the most significant abiding passions of his life. Essentially a humble man Michael Faraday actually turned down the offer of a Knighthood from Queen Victoria. He also turned down the Presidency of the Royal Society, twice. One of its previous presidents, Sir Joseph Banks had refused, of course, to even have the young Faraday as a bottle-washer.

In 1864 Michael was invited to become President of the Royal Institution in honour of all he had done for it but he refused this honour too. Michael held memberships of more than fifty learned societies in the world and had accepted a Knighthood in the Prussian Order of Merit.

In the early 1860's as Michael was painfully aware of his declining powers, an important subject began to fill his thinking: the future life, which lay beyond death. Did his Christian faith help as his mind began to falter? It certainly did. On the 19th September, 1861 Michael wrote to his great friend the physicist Auguste de la Rive:

'I am, I hope, very thankful that in the withdrawal of the powers and things of this life – the good hope is left with me which makes the contemplation of death – a comfort – not a fear. Such peace is alone in the gift of God; and as it is He who gives it, why should we be afraid? His unspeakable gift in His beloved Son is the ground of no doubtful hope; – and there is the rest for those who like you and me are drawing near the latter end of our term here below … I am happy and content.'

His wife Sarah was a great comfort in these difficult times and he described her as being a pillow to his mind. By December 1863 Michael was referring to how his words tottered, his memory tottered, his legs tottered, and how he was 'a very tottering and helpless thing.' However his faith was anything but tottering, it made him, despite being frequently in pain, positively cheerful.

By 1865 he had completely retired from the laboratories at the Royal Institution and in February 1865 he wrote to the Compte de Paris, 'I bow before him who is Lord of all, and hope to be kept waiting patiently for His time and mode of releasing me.'

He now spent most of his time in his home in Hampton Court. He often repeated the 46th and

23rd Psalms. He loved to sit under the lime trees of Hampton Court and watch the sunset and always enjoyed standing at his window watching the dazzling effects of an electric storm worshipping the God who created it all.

When his physician, Dr. Henry Bence Jones visited Michael in Hampton Court in July 1866 he found it a deeply moving scene.

'How are you Professor Faraday?' said the doctor.

'I am waiting, just waiting,' replied Michael cheerfully.

'Yes, you are waiting,' replied the doctor.

'And you? Are you waiting?' asked Michael with tears now running down his cheeks.

'This week, doctor, my uncle has been quoting the first verse of Psalm 46,' explained Michael's niece, Jane Barnard who was standing by the bedside. "God is our refuge and strength, an ever-present help in trouble." '

'Who is Dr. Bence Jones's refuge and strength?' asked Michael turning to his niece.

The doctor was moved by the great Professor's question. In truth it is a question everyone should ask. If the Lord is our refuge and strength we will not fear, wrote the Psalmist "even though the earth be removed and though the mountain shake with its swelling."

Death was only a few months away and as Michael lay dying he was asked a question.

'What are your speculations Professor?'

'Speculations?' he asked in surprise. 'Speculations, I have none. I am resting on certainties. I know whom I have believed, and am persuaded that He is able to keep that which I have committed on to him against that day.'

For fifty years Michael had moved amidst the speculations of science but his soul did not rest on speculation. He wrote to his niece from his deathbed 'My faculties are slipping away day by day. Happy is it for all of us that our true good lies not in them. As they ebb, may they leave us as little children trusting in the Father of Mercies and accepting His unspeakable gift.'

The man who loved children approached death with a childlike faith. The man who had helped the scientific world make a seismic shift and who helped bring about the modern world as we know it 'had a standard of duty'. Dr. Bence Jones later wrote, that 'was not founded upon any ideas of right and wrong, nor was it fashioned upon any outward experiences of time and place; but it was founded entirely on what he held to be the written Word, and throughout all his life his faith led him to act up to every letter of it.' Michael trusted the God of the Bible. He knew that the Bible was true, every word of it, and that he could rely on his wonderful Creator.

On the afternoon of Sunday August 25th 1867 Michael Faraday died quietly, in his favourite armchair in his study at his residence at Hampton Court. Michael had specifically stated in his will that his burial might be 'conducted in a moderate, sober and inexpensive way.' His wishes were fulfilled. Five days later his body was taken from Hampton Court to the Royal Institution where the carriages paused for a moment outside the building where he had made such an incredible impact. Soon the carriages crossed Oxford Street not far away from 18 Weymouth Street where Sir Humphry Davy's carriages had first picked Michael up and swept him away to an incredible new life. The funeral procession continued on up the hill to Highgate Cemetery where Michael's body was laid to rest.

Michael's wife Sarah lived for another twelve years and died in January 1879. Michael's relationship with Sarah that had begun so slowly when she was only nineteen years of age had grown into a very successful marriage. The world owes Sarah a great debt for the support and encouragement she gave to her incredible husband. How incredible is best summed up in the words of the scientist John Tyndall: 'Michael Faraday was the greatest experimental philosopher the world has ever seen: and I will add the opinion, that the progress of future research will tend, not to dim or diminish, but to enhance the labours of this mighty investigator.'

Michael Faraday's method of showing the workings of natural forces and their effects is used in schools and universities to this day. His discoveries have had an incalculable effect on all subsequent scientific and technical development. He was a genius who enthusiastically gave God all the glory for his remarkable life. His mother used to say with affection 'My Michael!' but we now say with the same affection 'our Michael!' because Michael Faraday belongs to the ages.

Bibliography

This list is intended to indicate the principal works from which the author has drawn in his research, to acknowledge his debt to their authors as well as to provide some suggestions for further reading.

Hamilton, James, *Faraday; The Life*, Harper Collins Publishers, London, 2002.

Morus, Twan Rhys, *Michael Faraday and the Electrical Century*, Icon Books Limited, Cambridge, 2004.

Griffin, John and Mary, *Faraday in 90 minutes*, Constable and Company Limited, London, 1997.

Cantor, Geoffrey, *Michael Faraday; Sandemanian and Scientist*, Macmillan, 1991.

Bragg, Melvyn, *Twelve Books That Changed the World*, Hodder and Stoughton, 2006

The author wishes to thank Dorothy Boyd for her enthusiastic and most encouraging help in preparing the manuscript of this book for publication. He also wishes to thank Ian McClure, B.Sc for his help regarding the scientific aspects of this book. Ian even went to the trouble of brilliantly demonstrating some of Michael's experiments to the author in order to show him the significance of Professor Faraday's work.

Michael Faraday, Timeline
1791 - 1867

1752	The first general hospital is founded in Philadelphia, in America
	Benjamin Franklin invents the lightning rod
1753	Foundation of the British Museum
1755	Publication of *Johnson's Dictionary*
1776	David Bushnell invents the submarine
1775-1783	The American War of Independence
1791	Michael Faraday born
1797	The first £1 banknotes introduced
1801	The first British census
1803-1815	The Napoleonic Wars
1805	The Battle of Trafalgar
1807	The Abolition of the Slave Trade
1811	Publication of Jane Austin's *Sense and Sensibility*
1821	Faraday marries Sarah Barnard
	Faraday makes a public profession of his faith in Jesus Christ
	Faraday publishes a paper in *The Annals of Philosophy*
	Faraday begins work at his bench in the Royal Institution
	Faraday develops the first electric motor
1823	The Royal Academy of Music opens
1824	George IV encourages the creation of the National Gallery
1825	Faraday isolates benzene
1831	Faraday discovers the induction of electric currents and develops the dynamo

1832	Publication of Tennyson's *Lady of Shalot*
1833	Children in the United Kingdom, under 9 years of age, are prohibited from working in mills
1837	Queen Victoria ascends throne
	Faraday demonstrates that electrostatic force consists of a field of curved lines of force
1840	Introduction of the Penny Black stamp
1842	Crawford Long performs the first operation using ether-based anaesthesia
1845	Faraday discovers The Faraday effect: an intense magnetic field can rotate the plane of polarized light
1848	The first U.K. Public Health Act. This provided a central board of health with powers to supervise street cleaning, refuse collection, water supply and sewerage disposal
1851	The Great Exhibition
1854-1856	The Crimean War
1857	The Indian Mutiny
	E Graves Otis demonstrates his invention of a passenger elevator
1858	Faraday publishes, *Experimental Researches in Chemistry and Physics*
1860	Faraday publishes *The Chemical History of a Candle* from his children's lectures
1867	Michael Faraday dies

Life Summary:
Michael Faraday

Today Faraday is recognised as one of the greatest experimental scientists in history. Much of our modern every day lives has been deeply influenced by him.

Faraday was a genius but his greatest characteristic was that he was devoted to the Lord Jesus. He served his Lord faithfully at the centre of the European scientific community. He is the only scientist to ever appear on the British £20 pound note!

The son of a blacksmith, Faraday was born in London in 1791. He was apprenticed to a bookbinder and this fostered within him a love of reading. His strong interest in science moved Faraday to apply for a job to Humphry Davy. In 1813 he became Davy's assistant and spent the next eighteen months touring Europe in order to investigate Davy's theory of volcanic action. After Davy's retirement in 1827, Faraday replaced him as Professor of Chemistry at the Royal Institution.

Faraday's greatest contribution to science was in the field of electricity. In 1821 he began experimenting with electromagnetism and invented the electric motor. In 1831 Faraday discovered the induction of electric currents and made the first dynamo. In 1837 he demonstrated that electrostatic force consists of a field of curved lines of force and conceived a specific inductive capacity. This led to Faraday being able to develop his theories on light and gravitational systems.

The government recognized his contribution to science by granting him a pension and a house in Hampton Court. However, Faraday was unwilling to use his knowledge to help military action and in 1853 refused to help develop poison gases for the Crimean War. He died in 1867.

Thinking Further Topics

Switch on the Light

When you think of all the things that Michael Faraday discovered – it is simply amazing.

Take a look around the room where you are at the moment and see how many things there are which owe something to this eminent scientist and his work.

Now stop a minute – look at your world. Think how there is nothing that exists outside the power of the almighty God and Creator.

He has made everything – and he has done it very well.

He has made rocks and elements and gasses and minerals and electrodes and mammals and fish. He has given living organisms the ability to reproduce. He has made life!

That is our great and wonderful God! The God who understands science perfectly because he invented it.

He knows the truth – the truth that we are just beginning to discover.

Isaiah 40:26
'Lift your eyes and look to the heavens:
Who created all these?
He who brings out the starry host one by one,
and calls them each by name.'

Mike

We all begin somewhere, we all have a past, ancestors, family. We all have to learn to adapt to life. We all have things we are good at and not so good at.

Life has a whole set of problems to throw at us – sometimes we may wish that these problems didn't exist. Sometimes we think that other people seem to be so much better off. They never seem to struggle with anything. If you'd seen Faraday give one of his famous lectures you might have thought that he'd had a great life. He was a brilliant scientist and people respected him, but in actual fact Michael came from very difficult beginnings and he still had problems later on. His life wasn't easy. His parents were poor, there was often a shortage of food. Michael suffered from dyslexia and a speech impediment.

Sometimes problems are opportunities for you to become a stronger person. Sometimes they are sent to test us. Sometimes it is simply a fact of life. Sin in the world causes pain and hardship. So what is the best way to cope with problems?

Faraday found that trusting in God was a great help. We don't know when he became a Christian but later on in life we know that he was. Faraday trusted in the one true God, the Creator. He believed in the Lord Jesus Christ, God's son.

You should trust in him too. Ask God to take your life and make it into something glorious for him.

Psalm 34:3
'Glorify the Lord with me; let us exalt his name together.'

Little Things Lead to Big Things

Remember that God is in control. Michael Faraday had a poor upbringing. He had one loaf of bread which had to last him a week. It was amazing that he got an education let alone became a famous scientist. However, God is in control! Remember that! He was in control of Michael's life and he is in control of yours.

Michael Faraday was grateful for the job as an apprentice bookbinder. It was a wonderful opportunity and his boss was keen to help Faraday learn and develop his skills. Think about your skills and abilities. How can you develop them? What about your mind? Do you long to learn more; to stretch it and see it gain knowledge?

God gave you a mind as a great gift. Above all he wants you to keep your mind pure. He wants you to think about those things that are pure and lovely and not to dirty your mind with wrong and evil thoughts.

Use it to study and to think. Use it to discover God. But be careful not to use it in ways that would dishonour the God who created it.

Romans 12:2
'Do not conform any longer to the pattern of this world; but be transformed by the renewing of your mind. Then you will be able to test and approve what God's will is – his good, pleasing and perfect will.'

Fire-lighter, Sweeper, and Washer

Michael had many blessings in his life – one of his blessings was good friends.

This is something of great importance, particularly to young people. Your whole life's path can be determined by the company you keep.

There is the saying that 'Bad company corrupts good character.'

There is also a verse in the Bible that says, 'There is a friend who sticks closer than a brother' Proverbs 18:24.

In John 15:13 it tells us 'Greater love has no one than this, that he laid down his life for his friends.'

Jesus has done this and more – he gave his life for sinners. He did this so that they would be saved from eternal death.

Choose your friends and your company wisely but most of all choose Christ.

Deuteronomy 30:19
'I have set before you life and death, blessings and curses. Now choose life, so that you and your children may live.'

The Man who had Never Seen the Sea

Faraday knew what it was like to have people against him because of his social background.

Lady Davy wasn't that keen on him and took every opportunity to 'put him in his place'.

Later on in life Faraday had to face similar opposition from colleagues and other scientists.

Humility was his great defence in these difficult times. Faraday didn't dwell on the pain and hurt. Later in life he thought more about Christ and wished to give him the glory.

Jesus Christ is the greatest example of true humility that we have. The Son of God came from the glory and power of heaven to be a helpless baby. Then after he had spent his life ministering to people, healing the sick and raising people from the dead – he was nailed to a cross to die. He was falsely accused of things that he hadn't done and sentenced to a shameful and degrading death. This wasn't, however, a straightforward miscarriage of justice or a murder. Jesus chose to die in order to save his people from their sins. He was God and man yet he was willing to suffer the humiliating death on the cross so that eternal life could be given freely to those who believed in him.

Luke 22:26
'The greatest among you should be like the youngest, and the one who rules like the one who serves.'

Over the Hills and Far Away

Faraday's travels took him much further than he had ever travelled before. This wasn't hard though as he had only ever been ten miles out of London in his whole life.

Michael saw the people of Rome celebrate the resurrection, on the same trip he wanted to purchase a Bible for himself. Something was stirring in Michael's heart and soul. Do you ever feel as if there is something touching your soul, trying to change you, trying to help you understand more about God? Do you ever feel drawn towards finding out more about God?

Perhaps you have questions about the Bible or about life after death? Don't ignore these thoughts. Don't dismiss them as not worth thinking about. God is at work in your heart and these thoughts and questions are the Holy Spirit working in you. Pray to God, read the Bible and share your thoughts and questions with other people who believe in God and read his Word.

Hebrews 4:7
'Today if you hear his voice; do not harden your heart.'

Not Every Girl Likes a Windmill

Michael fell in love and persuaded Sarah to marry him. She hadn't been that keen at first but she grew to understand him. Perhaps you're not keen on God? Perhaps you just don't understand all this 'faith' and 'Christianity'? Perhaps you don't believe at all?

Just because you don't believe doesn't mean that God has given up on you. He is full of mercy and doesn't want anyone to perish.

God can be at work in your life gradually. He can change things slowly but surely. Over time he can bring you to trust in him. So you could realise one day that 'Yes, I do believe in Jesus. He died to save ME from MY sins.' You may never be sure of when it actually happened. Some people are like that – they don't know when, they just know that God has changed them.

If this has happened to you then praise God that he has saved you from sin. If not – then ask God to save you now. Jesus has said, 'Come to me and be saved.' If you come to Christ and ask him to save you he will. Being saved does not depend on you and how you feel. You might wonder sometimes if you really are saved. Just remember that salvation depends on Christ alone. Ask him to save you. He will. He has promised. He is faithful. Believe in him.

You may come even if you are struggling with unbelief. Ask the Lord to help you overcome your unbelief. He has done this before - he will do it for you too.

Mark 9:24
'Immediately the boy's father exclaimed, "I do believe; help me overcome my unbelief." '

Curious and Important

We all have good sides and bad sides. Sometimes if we do not control ourselves the bad side gains importance over the good.

Michael had outbursts of joy, but was also known to have a fiery temper. But with God's grace Michael managed to keep it under control even when he was treated unjustly.

Jesus Christ was treated unjustly. Jealous men plotted against him, they accused him falsely and then sentenced him to death on a cross. But even as he suffered this cruel death he prayed for those men who hurt him.

'Father forgive them for they know not what they do.'

Faraday's life took on the characteristics of Christ the more he submitted himself to Christ.

Submit yourself to Christ and ask him to make your life one that honours God.

1 Samuel 2:30
'Those who honour me I will honour.'

A Very Special Candle at Christmas

Faraday told the young people at his lectures to 'shine as lights to those about you.'

Someone once said that 'All it takes for evil to prosper is for good men to do nothing.'

If you believe in Christ you should stand against evil, defend the poor, fight injustice, witness to the truth of God's Word.

A small match lit on a dark night can be seen from miles away.

Your life, though young and possibly inexperienced can show the world the truth of Jesus Christ. Any life, young or old can do this if they have submitted to Jesus and trusted in him for salvation.

Your actions and your life must back up your words. There is no point in saying you follow Christ when your actions do not show this. Greed, jealousy, backbiting and angry words, a complaining nature, selfish desires and lustful thoughts – these are not a reflection of Jesus Christ. If we see them in our lives we should fight our sinful natures to get rid of them. With God's help we can.

1 Timothy 6:9
'People who want to get rich fall into temptation and
a trap and into many foolish and harmful desires that
plunge men into ruin and destruction.'

The Father of Electricity

To be truly Christian is not something that is weak and spineless. It is hard work and needs spiritual strength. Jesus teaches us to 'turn the other cheek' when someone hurts us. This means that we don't try to get back at them, we don't try to hurt them because they hurt us. We pray for them. This goes against the selfish and sinful nature that human beings have.

It can take us a lifetime to become like Christ and to learn to put others before ourselves and God first of all. It will take our lifetime for God to make us into the people he wants us to be. No one is ever sinless in this life – and it is only when believers in Christ die and go to heaven that they are free of sin.

So believe in the Lord Jesus Christ and you will be saved. Be sure to believe. Then ask God for the strength to see you through to the end – to that time when God decides to bring you to heaven.

Psalm 28:7
'The Lord is my strength and my shield.
My heart trusts in him and I am helped.'

Reaching for the Stars

Lady Lovelace described Faraday as someone who was 'ever willing to serve man as under God, but not to serve man instead of God.'

Serving others is something that Jesus shows us how to do in his Word. He came to this world to serve and not to be served. That's quite unusual for someone as powerful as he is. Usually in this world it is the powerful people who demand service from others – but Jesus Christ operates differently.

It is good to know that in serving others we also serve God.

He knows our weaknesses, abilities, strengths. He knows what time we have and if we are busy, too busy or quiet.

Serving others should always be a part of serving God. He should be first in our lives.

Mark 12:30
'Love the Lord your God with all your heart,
with all your soul, and with all your mind
and with all your strength.'

Nothing is too Wonderful

Are you waiting? Are you waiting for God in your life? Are you patient enough to stand back and say – "God knows best. I will let him choose what should happen in my life and when it should happen,"? Do you ask God to guide you in your decisions? Do you read his Word and spend time in prayer and quiet before God, waiting on his instructions?

Are you waiting for God to make you into the person he wants you to be? Are you longing for that time when you will see Jesus face to face? Do you wait patiently for God's timing, for that day when he will take you to heaven and where sin will be no more?

Wait on God in good times and bad. Trust in him. Ask him for the forgiveness of your sins. Look at what Jesus did to save sinners on the cross. Ask him to save you. You won't have to wait for that. Salvation comes to those who ask for it and Jesus has never turned any one away.

Psalm 46:1
'God is our refuge and strength
an ever present help in trouble.'

TRAILBLAZERS

These are excellent books which give good role models to young people. Throughout history Christians have been in the forefront of new ideas and adventures; travel and social justice as well as struggling against dictatorships and persecution. These men and women from the past and the present not only show us how to live our lives, but also bring us closer to God.

John Calvin, After Darkness Light
ISBN 978-1-84550-084-9
John Newton, A Slave Set Free
ISBN 978-1-85792-834-1
Billy Graham, Just Get Up Out Of Your Seat
ISBN 978-1-84550-095-5

Patricia St. John, The Story Behind the Stories
ISBN 978-1-84550-328-4
Helen Roseveare, On His Majesty's Service
ISBN 978-1-84550-259-1

CHRISTIAN FOCUS PUBLICATIONS

Christian Focus | Christian Heritage | CF4K | Mentor

Christian Focus Publications publishes books for adults and children under its four main imprints: Christian Focus, Christian Heritage, CF4K and Mentor. Our books reflect that God's word is reliable and Jesus is the way to know him, and live for ever with him.

Our children's publication list includes a Sunday school curriculum that covers pre-school to early teens; puzzle and activity books. We also publish personal and family devotional titles, biographies and inspirational stories that children will love.

If you are looking for quality Bible teaching for children then we have an excellent range of Bible story and age specific theological books.

From pre-school to teenage fiction, we have it covered!

Find us at our web page:
www.christianfocus.com

CF4•K
Because you're never
too young to know Jesus